Getting Started with

MS-DOS® 5

and the *New* MS-DOS Shell

Getting Started with
MS-DOS® 5
and the *New* MS-DOS Shell

Carl Townsend

PUBLISHED BY
Microsoft Press
A Division of Microsoft Corporation
One Microsoft Way
Redmond, Washington 98052-6399

Copyright © 1991 by Carl Townsend

All rights reserved. No part of the contents of this book
may be reproduced or transmitted in any form or by any means
without the written permission of the publisher.

Library of Congress Cataloging-in-Publication Data

Townsend, Carl, 1938–
   Getting started with MS-DOS 5 and the new MS-DOS shell / Carl
Townsend.
      p.   cm. -- (Getting started right)
   Includes index.
   ISBN 1-55615-353-8
   1. MS-DOS (Computer operating system) I. Title. II. Title:
Getting started with MS-DOS five and the new MS-DOS shell.
III. Series.
QA76.76.063T694   1991
005.4'46--dc20   91-10309
                                                                         CIP

Printed and bound in the United States of America.

1 2 3 4 5 6 7 8 9   AGAG   6 5 4 3 2 1

Distributed to the book trade in Canada by Macmillan of Canada, a division of
Canada Publishing Corporation.

Distributed to the book trade outside the United States and Canada by Penguin Books Ltd.

Penguin Books Ltd., Harmondsworth, Middlesex, England
Penguin Books Australia Ltd., Ringwood, Victoria, Australia
Penguin Books N.Z. Ltd., 182-190 Wairau Road, Auckland 10, New Zealand

British Cataloging-in-Publication Data available.

IBM®, PC/AT®, and PS/2® are registered trademarks and PC/XT™ is a trademark of
International Business Machines Corporation. PC Tools™ is a trademark of Central
Point Software, Inc. Microsoft® and MS-DOS® are registered trademarks and
QBasic™ and Windows™ are trademarks of Microsoft Corporation.

Acquisitions Editor: Michael Halvorson
Manuscript Editor: Pat Coleman
Project Editor: Mary Renaud
Technical Editor: Gerald Joyce

Contents

Introduction   vii

Chapter 1   A Tour of the Shell   1
Chapter 2   Managing Files   19
Chapter 3   Managing Disks   35
Chapter 4   Managing Directories   49
Chapter 5   Running Applications   63
Chapter 6   At the Command Prompt   79
Chapter 7   Protecting Your Data   97
Chapter 8   Introduction to the Editor   111
Chapter 9   The Basics of Batch Files   123
Chapter 10   Customizing Your System   133

Appendix A   Installing DOS 5   151
Appendix B   Glossary   155
Appendix C   Keyboard and Mouse Conventions   165
Appendix D   Troubleshooting   169
Appendix E   Recommended Reading   177

Index   181

Introduction

If you are new to personal computing and DOS, *Getting Started with MS-DOS 5 and the* New *MS-DOS Shell* is the first book you need.

If you are an occasional computer user who is ready to install DOS 5 or upgrade to DOS 5 from an earlier version of DOS, this might be the only DOS book you need.

Getting Started with MS-DOS 5 and the New *MS-DOS Shell* provides a hands-on approach that leads you step by step through the basics. Flip through this book, and you'll notice a lot of practices. These are exercises with numbered steps that show you exactly how to do the things you do almost every time you use your computer:

- Find and run an application program
- Copy files to and from a floppy disk
- Rename a file
- Delete a file
- Make a directory
- Change directories
- View the contents of a file
- Print a file

If you are a new computer user, start with Chapter 1 and simply work straight through the book. If you have some previous experience with DOS, you can refresh your memory by looking up a practice, checking on a command, or reviewing the tips at the end of each chapter.

ABOUT THE NEW MS-DOS SHELL

The Shell is the quick and easy way to learn and use DOS. You can use it for almost all your daily operating system chores. You can access it with the keyboard or with a mouse. Depending on your hardware, you can run the Shell in text mode (alphanumeric characters only) or graphics mode (pictures and alphanumeric characters).

If you have not yet installed DOS 5, do so by following the instructions in Appendix A and in your DOS manual. You can set up your system so that either the Shell or the DOS command prompt appears whenever you start or restart your computer. If you are a new user, you should choose to have the Shell appear.

If you have a mouse, using the Shell is really easy—and fast. For example, if you want to copy a file from drive C to drive A, simply click on the filename and drag it to the icon (in graphics mode) or the drive letter (in text mode) that represents drive A. By the time you release the mouse button, the file is copied.

Using the Shell with the keyboard is a bit more involved. In this book, instructions are given for both mouse and keyboard. Appendix C summarizes some of the most helpful conventions and shortcuts you can use with the mouse and the keyboard.

THE COMMAND PROMPT

Before the Shell, there was the DOS command prompt—the funny drive letter with the blinking cursor next to it. The command prompt always seems a bit daunting to new users: You have to know which commands do what, you have to type the commands correctly, and you have to remember them. The Shell does most of this for you. Files, commands, and options are displayed on the screen, and you simply select the ones you want.

But because working with the command prompt is such an integral part of DOS, and because you still need to use the command prompt for certain tasks, this book contains a chapter on how to use it (Chapter 6). If you are in a hurry to get started with the Shell, you can leave this chapter for a later session, but do work through it. It will give you a better idea of the inner workings of DOS.

FURTHER HELP

You don't need much experience with computers to use this book. Computer terms and procedures are carefully explained as they are introduced in the text. But if you are puzzled by a term and need a reminder, you can quickly check the glossary found in Appendix B.

What if you run into a problem while you are working with the Shell? The Shell itself contains comprehensive Help information (discussed in Chapter 1) about almost every feature. Or you can consult Appendix D, a troubleshooting guide that identifies some common problems and suggests ways to solve them.

When you've mastered the basics of working with the Shell, you might want to tackle some of DOS 5's advanced features. Appendix E recommends some books that can help you become a more proficient user of DOS and that also offer you a fascinating look into the world of personal computing.

Chapter 1

A Tour of the Shell

DOS (Disk Operating System) is a set of programs that manages the resources in an IBM PC or compatible computer. MS-DOS is the operating system first released by Microsoft in 1981. Since that time, it has been through several revisions, the latest being Microsoft MS-DOS operating system version 5. New features in this version include the ability to make more memory available to programs and a new MS-DOS Shell.

When the computer is turned off, MS-DOS resides on a disk as a set of files. When you turn on the computer, MS-DOS is loaded from the disk, and control of the computer is given to the user.

You use MS-DOS when you format and copy disks, examine disk directories, or copy files, for example. The MS-DOS Shell simplifies these and other tasks and thus helps you become productive on your computer more quickly.

WHAT IS THE MS-DOS SHELL?

The operating system is the heart of computer software, and it communicates directly with the computer hardware. At the next level is the MS-DOS Shell—an operating environment.

If you are a new user of the computer, you'll find the Shell handy. For example, you can copy a file without knowing the name of the program that copies files, how to spell the program name, where it is located, or how to use it. Simply select the file you want to copy, and then choose the word Copy from a menu. The Shell asks where you want to copy the file and then copies the file for you.

You can use the Shell to start programs, to manage your disks and files, and to switch quickly between executing programs. This chapter walks you through the steps involved in starting the Shell, choosing commands, and quitting the Shell.

NOTE: This book assumes that you have already installed MS-DOS 5 and the MS-DOS Shell. If you have not, do so by following the instructions found in your MS-DOS manual and in Appendix A of this book.

STARTING THE SHELL

Depending on how you install MS-DOS 5, the Shell will either start each time you turn on the computer (or when you reboot) or start only upon request.

Turn on the computer (or reboot). You will see either the command prompt or the Shell window.

- If you see the command prompt (C:\>), you must start the Shell with a specific command. Type the following command and then press Enter:

DOSSHELL

- If you see a window similar to Figure 1-1, the Shell is at your service.
- If the Shell doesn't start, verify that you have the correct version of DOS (MS-DOS version 5) by typing the following command at the command prompt and then pressing Enter:

VER

 NOTE: When typing text at the command prompt, you can use either uppercase or lowercase letters. MS-DOS (or simply DOS, for short) is not sensitive to letter case.

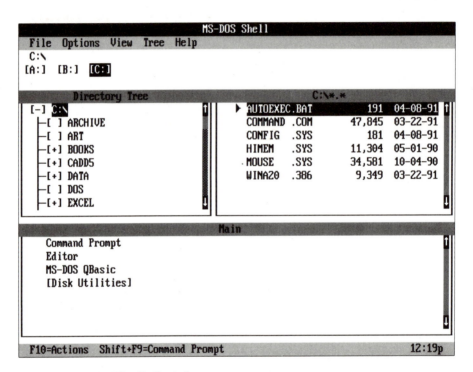

FIGURE 1-1. *The Shell window.*

THE SHELL WINDOW

The Shell window is divided into several areas and offers some helpful features, as shown in Figure 1-2.

Chapter 1: A Tour of the Shell

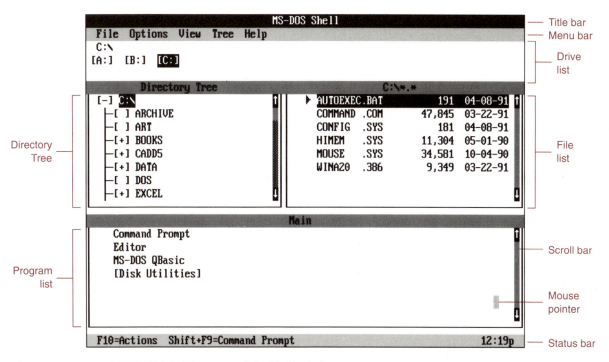

FIGURE 1-2. *The areas of the Shell window.*

- The *title bar* displays the name of the program (MS-DOS Shell).

- The *menu bar* displays menus that are currently available.

- From the *drive list*, the *Directory Tree*, and the *File list*, you define and select the material you want to work with.

- The *Program list* shows the names of other programs installed to run easily from the Shell.

- If you have a mouse, you will see a *mouse pointer*—a small rectangle (in text mode) or an arrow (in graphics mode)—on the screen. You can use the mouse with the *scroll bars* to vertically scroll the contents of windows.

- The *status bar* displays some available keystrokes, Shell messages, and the current time as defined by the system clock.

You work in one area of the Shell window at a time. Use the Tab key to move to another area, or click the mouse pointer in an area to make it active.

USING THE SHELL

Selecting and choosing are the basic operations in using the Shell. Selecting an item causes the item to be highlighted. Choosing causes an action to be executed. You can use the mouse or the keyboard to select or choose. Practices in this book assume your familiarity with the techniques of selecting and choosing.

Selecting and Choosing with the Mouse

- To select any item in the Shell window, simply click on the item—that is, position the mouse pointer on the item, and then press and release the mouse button once. When the item is highlighted, it is selected. For example, to select a directory in the Directory Tree, click on its name.
- To cancel a selection, select another item.
- To choose an item, double-click on the item—that is, position the mouse pointer on the item, and press the mouse button twice quickly.

NOTE: With the mouse, selecting an item from the drive list or from a menu is the same as choosing the item. You can only select items—not choose them—in the Directory Tree.

Selecting and Choosing with the Keyboard

- To select an area of the window, tab to it.
- To select an item in an area, use the arrow keys. To move a full list at a time, press PgUp or PgDn.
- To cancel a selection, select another item.
- To choose an item, select it and then press Enter.

USING MENUS

In the Shell, you issue commands by choosing them from menus. Command names are listed on menus using the following conventions:

Chapter 1: A Tour of the Shell

Command followed by ellipsis (...)	This command will initiate the display of a dialog box.
Command preceded by diamond (♦)	This command is a toggle (turns a command on or off) and is currently toggled on.
Command followed by key combination	These keystrokes are a shortcut for the command.
Command name shaded or missing	This command is not currently available for use.

Menus and the Mouse

To use the mouse with a menu, first be sure the desired screen area is active.

- Click on the name in the menu bar to display a menu, and then click on the desired command.

- To cancel a menu, click on the menu name or click anywhere outside the menu.

Menus and the Keyboard

To use the keyboard with a menu, first press Alt or F10 to activate the menu bar. You can then choose a command using either of these methods:

- Use the Left or Right arrow key to select the desired menu name. Press Enter to open the menu. Press the Up or Down arrow key to select the desired command, and then press Enter.

- Press the first letter of the menu name to display the menu. Press the underlined letter of the desired command. After a menu is open, you can move to adjacent menus by using the Left and Right arrow keys.

To close a menu without choosing a command, press Esc.

USING DIALOG BOXES

Shell commands that initiate a dialog box are indicated by an ellipsis (...) on the menu. For example, to display a sample dialog box, choose Run from the File menu. Figure 1-3 on the next page shows the dialog box that appears.

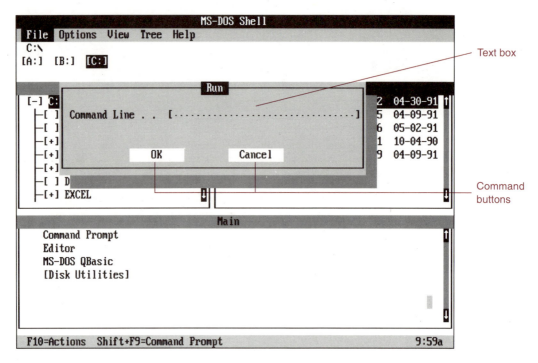

FIGURE 1-3. *The Run dialog box.*

This dialog box contains an input area called a text box. It also contains command buttons, labeled OK and Cancel, which initiate immediate action.

Text Boxes

You can edit text in a text box with the mouse or with the keyboard.

Practice:
Editing text with the mouse

1. At the insertion point in the Run dialog box, type this text:

   MEM

2. Position the mouse pointer on the area you want to edit, and hold down the mouse button.

3. Now drag the mouse to highlight the entire block of text to be edited, and then release the mouse button. Press Del to delete the text, or type new characters to replace the highlighted characters.

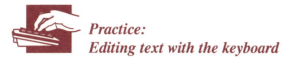

Practice:
Editing text with the keyboard

1. At the insertion point in the Run dialog box, type this text:

   MEM

2. To edit the text, you can use any of the keys shown in Figure 1-4.

Keystroke	Action
Home	Moves the cursor to the first character in the text box
End	Moves the cursor to the last character in the text box
Left arrow	Moves the cursor one character left
Right arrow	Moves the cursor one character right
Backspace	Deletes the character to the left of the cursor
Del	Deletes the character above the cursor
Tab	Moves the cursor between the text box and the command buttons

FIGURE 1-4. *Keystrokes for editing dialog boxes.*

You can also select characters by holding down the Shift key and moving the cursor with the arrow keys to highlight the characters. Press Del to delete the highlighted characters, or type replacement characters and press Enter.

NOTE: If the text box is full and you continue to enter characters, they will scroll to the left. Some dialog boxes have multiple text boxes. Use the Tab key to move the cursor forward between text boxes and buttons, and use Shift+Tab (hold down Shift while you press Tab) to move the cursor backward. You can also use the arrow keys.

Command Buttons

Most dialog boxes have two or more command buttons:

- To initiate action (execute a command), choose OK or press Enter.
- To cancel the action or command, choose Cancel or press Esc.

- To get help with the command, choose Help or press F1. Not all dialog boxes have a Help button.

You need to click the mouse button only once to choose a command button. You can choose a command button with the keyboard by using the Tab key to move the cursor to the command button and then pressing Enter.

*Practice:
Using command buttons*

1. With the Run dialog box still displayed, be sure the text you typed (MEM) still appears on the text line.

2. Click on OK or press Enter. The dialog box closes, the Shell disappears, and the MEM program executes, displaying information about the memory of your system and then allowing you to return to the Shell:

```
  655360 bytes total conventional memory
  655360 bytes available to MS-DOS
  588624 largest executable program size

 3145728 bytes total contiguous extended memory
       0 bytes available contiguous extended memory
  983040 bytes available XMS memory
         MS-DOS resident in High Memory Area

Press any key to return to MS-DOS Shell.....
```

Options

Some dialog boxes offer options, which are selected in one of these ways:

- Round option buttons indicate mutually exclusive options—you can select only one of them. The current selection is marked with a black dot.

- Square check boxes indicate that multiple options can be selected. Selected items are marked with an X, which is inserted or deleted by clicking on the check box or by pressing Spacebar when the cursor is in the check box.

Chapter 1: A Tour of the Shell

Practice:
Selecting dialog box options with the mouse

1. Click anywhere in the File list area.

2. Click on Options in the menu bar to open the Options menu.

3. Click on the File Display Options command. The File Display Options dialog box appears:

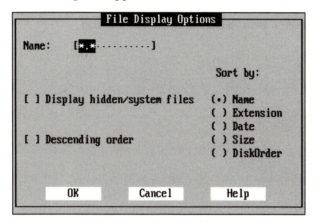

4. By default, filenames are sorted in alphabetic order. To change the order to date of creation or date last changed, click on the Date option button.

5. Choose the OK command button. The File list now appears in order by date, the oldest files first.

To use the check box options at the left, select one or both.

Practice:
Selecting dialog box options with the keyboard

1. Press the Tab key until the File list area is active.

2. Press Alt and then O to open the Options menu. (In practices in this book, underlines indicate the keys to be pressed.)

3. Press F to choose the File Display Options command. The File Display Options dialog box appears (as shown above).

11

GETTING STARTED WITH MS-DOS 5 AND THE *NEW* MS-DOS SHELL

4. Press the Tab key three times to move the cursor to the option buttons labeled Sort by.

5. By default, filenames are sorted in alphabetic order. To change the order to date of creation or date last changed, use the Down arrow key to select the Date option button.

6. Press Enter. The File list now appears in order by date, the oldest files first.

List Boxes

Some dialog boxes contain list boxes from which you can choose an item.

- To choose an item from a list box with a mouse, click on the scroll arrows until the desired item is available, and then double-click on the item. You can also click once on the item and then click on the OK command button.

- To choose an item from a list box with the keyboard, use the Up or Down arrow key to scroll vertically until the desired item is highlighted, and then press Enter. You can also type the first letter of the item to jump to the item in the list.

*Practice:
Using a list box*

1. From the Options menu, choose Colors to see the Color Scheme dialog box. It contains the Current Scheme list box:

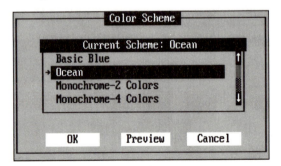

12

2. Eight color schemes are available:

Basic Blue	Reverse
Ocean	Hot Pink
Monochrome-2 Colors	Emerald City
Monochrome-4 Colors	Turquoise

3. Select any one of the color schemes, and then choose Preview to see if, for example, Hot Pink is for you. If it is, choose OK or press Enter. If not, choose Cancel.

THE PROGRAM LIST

The Program list contains four items: Command Prompt, Editor, MS-DOS QBasic, and Disk Utilities. These four make up the Main program group. Although you can add to this list (see Chapter 5), these four programs are present when you install the Shell.

- Command Prompt returns you to the DOS command prompt (C:\>), leaving the Shell in memory. At the DOS command prompt, you enter commands directly from the keyboard. (To return to the Shell when using the Command Prompt program, type *EXIT*—not *DOSSHELL*—at the prompt and press Enter.)

- Editor starts the Editor program. You can use the Editor to view or change text files.

- MS-DOS QBasic starts the QBasic interpreter. You can use QBasic to write your own programs.

- Disk Utilities is actually another group containing its own set of programs.

To start any program in the Program list, double-click on the program name, or select the name and press Enter.

Practice:
Exploring Disk Utilities

1. Move to the Program list area.

2. Choose Disk Utilities. Figure 1-5 shows the list of programs that are part of this group.

3. To return to the Main program group, press Esc or choose Main.

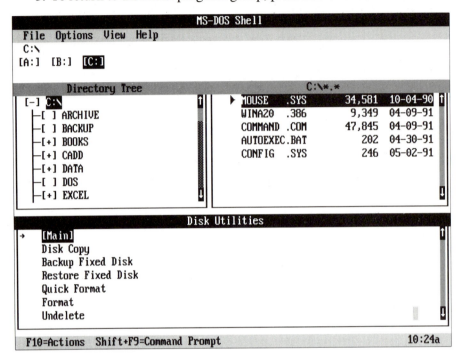

FIGURE 1-5. *The Disk Utilities program group in the Program list area.*

THE FILE LIST

The File list displays the names of the files in the current directory. You can use the File list area to start programs, but you must know the location of the program file. To start a program, first choose the drive and select the directory containing the program file. Choose the program name either by double-clicking on it or by highlighting it and pressing Enter. The program will then start. Another method is to first select the program and then choose Open from the File menu.

Practice:
Running a program

1. Select drive C from the drive list.

2. Move to the Directory Tree, and select the DOS directory. You will see a list of the files in this directory:

```
         C:\DOS\*.*
▶ 4201    .CPI      6,404  03-22-91
  4208    .CPI        720  03-22-91
  5202    .CPI        395  03-22-91
  ANSI    .SYS      9,029  03-22-91
  APPEND  .EXE     10,774  03-22-91
  APPNOTES.TXT      9,677  03-22-91
  ASSIGN  .COM      6,399  03-22-91
  ATTRIB  .EXE     15,796  03-22-91
```

3. Move to the File list area.

4. Press M to select the MEM program, and then press Enter to run it. Your screen displays information about the memory in your system, as shown on page 10.

5. Press any key to return to the Shell.

HELP!

When you are using the Shell and need assistance, select the item for which you need help and press F1. For example, to get help with the Confirmation command from the Options menu, press Alt and then O. (The Confirmation command is selected by default.) Then press F1, and a Help screen is displayed (Figure 1-6 on the next page). You can branch to other Help topics from this screen by using the command buttons. Press Esc or click on Close to return to the Shell.

You also will find a Help menu on the menu bar. The Index command on this menu displays a list of all Help topics, from which you can choose the desired topic. The other commands display Help information on selected subjects.

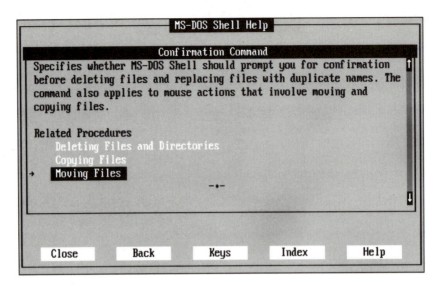

FIGURE 1-6. *A Help screen.*

DISPLAY MODE

The Shell runs in either text mode or graphics mode. Text mode uses text characters only—no pictures. The screen illustrations you've seen so far in this chapter are in text mode. Graphics mode uses text characters and graphical images. Figure 1-7 (on page 17) shows how the initial Shell window looks in graphics mode. You can compare it with Figure 1-1 to see the differences.

The rest of this book shows screens in graphics mode. You can use graphics mode if you have a CGA, an EGA, a VGA, or similar display. Let's now change from text mode to graphics mode.

Practice:
Selecting graphics mode

1. From the Options menu, choose Display.
2. In the Screen Mode dialog box, select the line Graphics 25 lines Low Resolution from the list box.
3. Choose OK or press Enter.

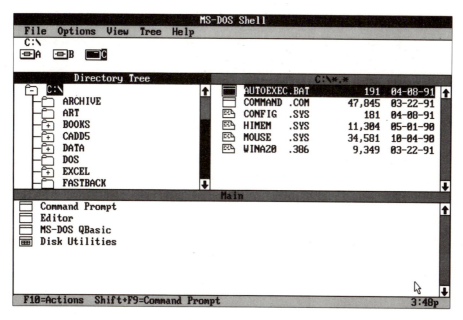

FIGURE 1-7. *The Shell window in graphics mode.*

QUITTING THE SHELL

You can quit the Shell at any time and return to the DOS prompt. To keep the Shell in memory while you run DOS temporarily, press Shift+F9 or choose Command Prompt from the Main program group in the Program list area to exit the Shell. You can return to the Shell at any time by typing *EXIT* at the DOS prompt and pressing Enter.

To exit the Shell and remove the Shell from memory, you can either press F3 or press Alt+F4, or you can choose Exit from the File menu. To return to the Shell after exiting with one of these methods, type *DOSSHELL* at the command prompt and press Enter.

NOTE: Try to keep track of how the Shell is loaded; you can end up with extra copies of the program in memory. If you choose Command Prompt from the Main program group or press Shift+F9 to exit the Shell, the Shell is still in memory but inactive. If you enter DOSSHELL at the DOS prompt now, a second copy of the Shell is loaded into memory.

Chapter 2

Managing Files

The information you work with is stored as data in the computer's memory. When you turn off the computer, this data is lost. To save data to use later, you must store it in a file on a disk. This chapter describes how to use the Shell to manage your files on a disk.

WHAT'S A FILE?

A file is any information stored as a single unit. A file could be a letter, a spreadsheet, a database of addresses, or an application program. (The DOS Shell is an application program stored as six separate files.)

When you start the Shell, a list of files in the current directory appears in the File list area (Figure 2-1). The filenames are in alphabetic order.

Files are stored in directories on a disk. Notice in Figure 2-1 that the icon next to a directory name is a file folder and that the icon next to a filename represents the contents of the file folder. (The icons are visible when the Shell is running in graphics mode.) Each directory has a unique name, and each file in each directory has a unique name. You will learn more about directories in Chapter 4.

To the right of the filenames in the File list are two columns. The first shows the size of the file in bytes. (A byte is the amount of disk space or memory needed to store a single character.) The second column shows the date the file was created or last modified.

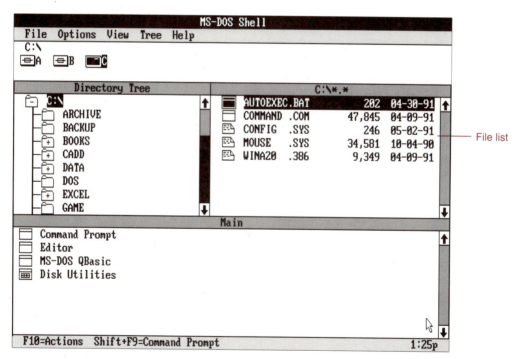

FIGURE 2-1. *The initial screen.*

FILENAMES

Filenames can be from one to eight characters. You can use letters, numbers, and any of the following symbols:

' ~ ! @ # $ % ^ & ( ) _ - { }

NOTE: Don't use periods, asterisks, question marks, or special characters other than those listed above in a filename. DOS reserves these for other purposes.

Filenames often have a suffix, called an extension, which indicates file type. The extension can be from one to three characters and is preceded by a period (usually referred to as "dot"). Here are some sample valid filenames:

F
OPM88.DBF
CUT&PAST.PCX
QU(1).DOC

Using Extensions
Many programs automatically add the proper extension when saving a file. For example, most word processors use a .DOC extension. In such cases, you need not add an extension to the filename when saving the file. When renaming, printing, viewing, or copying a file with the Shell, however, include the extension.

TYPES OF FILES

Most files are either program files or data files. Program files are computer instructions that are executed when you run a program. Program files typically have the extension .EXE or .COM. For example, DOSSHELL is stored on the disk as a collection of six program files.

Data files are files in which programs store information. The table at the top of the next page lists extensions for some sample types of data files:

Chapter 2: Managing Files

Extension	Type
.BAK	Backup file
.DOC	Document file for a word processor
.HLP	Help file
.TXT	Text file

MAKING SELECTIONS

Before you do anything with a file, you must first choose the drive containing the file, then select the directory containing the file, and finally select the file (or files). Basic selecting techniques are described in Chapter 1. The following practices show you how to select multiple items. If you want to cancel a multiple selection, choose Deselect All on the File menu, make another selection, or move the cursor.

Selecting with the Mouse

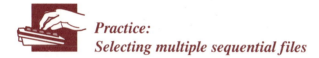
Practice:
Selecting multiple sequential files

1. In the File list area, click on the name of the first file to be selected.

2. Move the mouse pointer to the last filename you want to select.

3. Hold down Shift and click on the last filename.

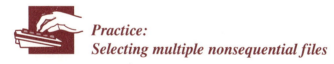
Practice:
Selecting multiple nonsequential files

1. In the File list area, click on the name of the first file to be selected.

2. Hold down Ctrl and click on each additional filename.

23

Selecting with the Keyboard

Practice:
Selecting multiple sequential files

1. In the File list area, use the arrow keys to select the first filename.
2. Hold down Shift and use the arrow keys to select the additional filenames.

Practice:
Selecting multiple nonsequential files

1. In the File list area, select the first filename. Then press Shift+F8 (hold down Shift while you press F8).
2. Move to the next filename to be selected, and press Spacebar.
3. To add other filenames, select each and press Spacebar.
4. Once again, press Shift+F8.

 To select multiple files across directories, choose Select Across Directories from the Options menu. To select all files in a directory, make the File list area active and then choose Select All from the File menu or press Ctrl+/(slash).

Shortcuts for Specifying File Groups

Using wildcard characters is often easier than selecting multiple files. The DOS wildcard characters are the asterisk (∗) and the question mark (?).

The asterisk represents any and all characters. For example, ∗.DOC specifies all files in the current directory that have the .DOC extension. Use ∗.∗ to specify all files in the current directory.

You can also use the asterisk to represent the last portion of the letters in the filename or extension. For example, BIRD∗.DOC includes BIRD1.DOC, BIRD2.DOC, and even BIRD10.DOC.

When you start the Shell, C:\∗.∗ appears at the top of the File list, indicating that the File list is displaying all files in the current directory. You can modify this display by specifying a different view. You can, for example, choose to display only those files in the current directory that have the .EXE filename extension.

Practice:
Entering a new view specification

1. From the Directory Tree, select the DOS directory.
2. From the Options menu, choose File Display Options.
3. In the Name box in the File Display Options dialog box, type:

   *.EXE

   and choose OK or press Enter.

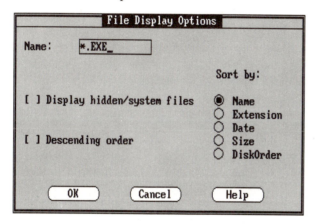

The File list now displays all the .EXE files in the current directory and only those files. To restore the original view, follow the steps above and type *.* in the Name box of the File Display Options dialog box.

NOTE: Changing the view does not delete files or change the directory in any way. Files are not deleted unless you use the Delete command from the File menu or press the Del key.

The other wildcard character is the question mark. You use it to ignore a *single* matching character in the filename. For example, BIRD?.DOC includes BIRD1.DOC, BIRD2.DOC, and so on (through BIRD9.DOC).

ORDERING THE FILE LIST

By default, filenames are sorted in alphabetic order. You can change the sort order by using the File Display Options command from the Options menu.

Practice:
Changing the sort order

1. From the Options menu, choose File Display Options.
2. Select the Extension option button in the dialog box:

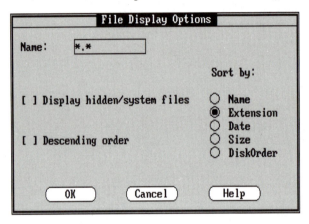

3. Choose OK or press Enter.

The filenames in the File list are now in alphabetic order by extension; filenames that have numeric extensions are listed first.

VIEWING FILES

You can use the Shell to view the contents of a file.

NOTE: You cannot edit the contents of a file displayed with the View File Contents command. Files that contain only text are displayed as normal text, but binary files (such as files with the .EXE or .COM extension) and files that contain any special coding (such as word processor document files) are displayed in hexadecimal code. To switch between a text or ASCII display and a hex display, use the Display menu or press F9.

Chapter 2: Managing Files

Practice:
Viewing the AUTOEXEC.BAT file

1. Select the root directory, and then select AUTOEXEC.BAT from the File list.

2. From the File menu, choose View File Contents, or press F9 to view the file's contents:

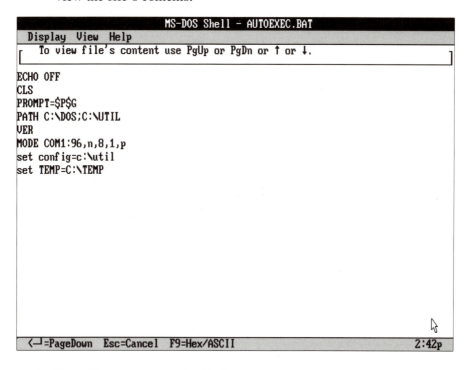

3. Press Esc to return to the Shell.

FINDING INFORMATION ABOUT A FILE

You can use the Shell to find specific information about a file or a group of files. Let's find information on all the Shell program files.

Practice:
Finding information about DOSSHELL

1. From the Directory Tree, select the DOS directory.

2. Move to the File list area, and then select all the files with the name DOSSHELL.

3. From the Options menu, choose Show Information. All the information about the DOSSHELL files is listed on the screen:

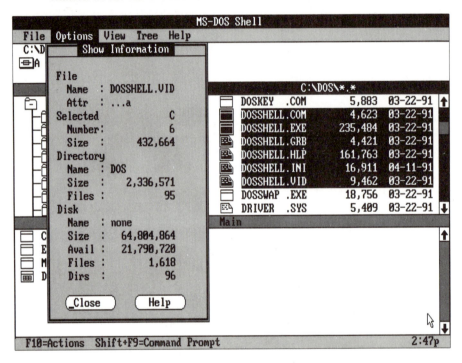

4. Choose Close or press Enter to return to a normal view.

Practice:
Finding information for all files on a disk

1. From the View menu, choose All Files.

2. Move to the File list area, and use the Down arrow key or the vertical scroll bar to move through this list.

3. From the View menu, choose Program/File Lists to return to a normal view.

BASIC FILE OPERATIONS

You can use the Shell to perform all basic file operations—finding, copying, moving, renaming, printing, and deleting.

Finding

Occasionally you might forget where you stored a file or even how you spelled the filename. You can use features of the Shell to locate such a file.

Practice:
Finding a file

1. From the File menu, choose Search.
2. In the Search File dialog box, type the filename or as much of it as you remember, using wildcard characters if necessary:

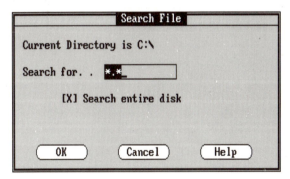

3. By default, DOS searches the entire disk. To search only the current directory, move to the Search entire disk check box and delete the X by pressing Spacebar or by clicking on the X.
4. Press Enter or choose OK. The Shell displays a Search Results window that lists all files matching the search criteria. You can select any of these files.

NOTE: A function that can be turned on or off is called a toggle. For example, you can toggle between searching the entire disk and searching only the selected directory by adding or deleting the X in the Search entire disk check box in the Search File dialog box.

Copying

When you copy a file, the original file remains as is and you create a duplicate in another place. You can copy a file from one directory to another and from one disk to another. You can even make a copy of a file within the same directory if you give the copy a different filename. (See ''Renaming,'' later in this chapter.)

Practice:
Copying with the mouse

    1. In the File list area, select the file (or files) to be copied.

    2. Hold down Ctrl and the mouse button, and drag the file to the directory where you want the copy to appear.

    3. Release the mouse button and then release Ctrl.

    4. In the Confirm Mouse Operation dialog box, choose Yes or press Enter.

The filename now appears in its new place in the File list as well as in its original place.

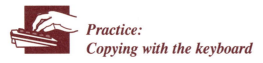
Practice:
Copying with the keyboard

    1. In the File list area, select the file (or files) to be copied.

    2. From the File menu, choose Copy, or press F8.

Chapter 2: Managing Files

3. In the Copy File dialog box, type the destination (the location where the copy should appear) in the To: field.

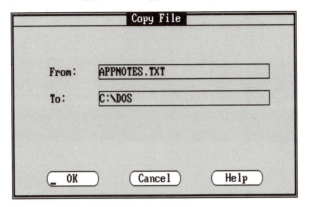

4. Choose OK or press Enter.

Moving

When you move a file, you physically take it from one place to another. You can move a file from one disk to another and from one directory to another. When you move a file, the filename is deleted from its original place in the File list and appears in its new location.

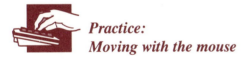
Practice:
Moving with the mouse

1. In the File list area, select the file (or files) to be moved.

2. Hold down the mouse button, and drag the selected file to the new location.

3. Release the mouse button.

4. In the Confirm Mouse Operation dialog box, choose Yes or press Enter.

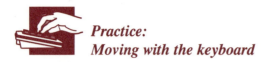

Practice:
Moving with the keyboard

1. In the File list area, select the file (or files) to be moved.
2. From the File menu, choose Move, or press F7.
3. In the Move File dialog box, type the destination in the To: field.
4. Choose OK or press Enter.

Renaming

You can change a filename as a single operation, or you can change a filename when you copy the file. To change a filename as part of copying, simply type the new name in the To: field of the Copy File dialog box. When you rename a file, its old name disappears from the File list, and its new name appears in the File list in the appropriate place.

Practice:
Renaming with the mouse or the keyboard

1. In the File list area, select the file to be renamed.
2. From the File menu, choose Rename.
3. In the Rename File dialog box, type the new name, including the extension.
4. Choose OK or press Enter.

Printing

You can print simple text files from the Shell—those with .BAT, .SYS, or .TXT extensions, for example—if you run the PRINT.COM utility before starting the Shell. (For information on PRINT.COM, see your DOS manual.) To print application files, however, such as a word processor document or a spreadsheet, use the application to print the file.

Chapter 2: Managing Files

Practice:
Printing with the mouse or the keyboard

1. In the File list area, select the file or files (a maximum of 10) to be printed.
2. From the File menu, choose Print.

Deleting

You should regularly delete files that you no longer need. Doing so keeps your disk neat and tidy and also helps you avoid running out of disk space.

Practice:
Deleting files with the mouse or the keyboard

1. In the File list area, select the file or files to be deleted.
2. From the File menu, choose Delete, or simply press Del.
3. In the Delete File Confirmation dialog box, choose OK or press Enter.

FILE MANAGEMENT TIPS

- Use filenames that identify the contents of the file. For example, if you are using a word processor to create a proposal for ACME Industries, choose ACME.DOC or ACMEPROP.DOC for the filename instead of PROP3.DOC.

- When naming or renaming a file, always use an extension. The extension should indicate the type of file. If you notice a filename without an extension, rename the file to include the extension.

- Name your files in a way that will simplify backing them up or deleting them. For example, if you are writing a book on birds, you might use BIRD1.DOC, BIRD2.DOC, BIRD3.DOC, and so on for chapter files. In this way, you can copy all the chapter files to a disk using the DOS command COPY with the wildcard filename BIRD?.DOC.

Chapter 3

Managing Disks

Disks are magnetic media devices that store data and programs. The two basic types of disks are hard (or fixed) disks and floppy disks (or diskettes). In this book, the term *disk* can refer to either a hard disk or a floppy disk.

Hard disks can store large amounts of data (20 megabytes to 40 megabytes or more) and can manage data quickly. Most users have a single physical hard disk. To manage disk space better, some users install DOS so that the computer recognizes a single physical disk as two or more logical disks. The first logical disk is drive C. Other logical disks are labeled consecutively as D, E, and F (or whatever is available). When you start the Shell, an identifier for each logical disk on your system appears near the top of the screen.

Floppy disks are removable platters that store programs and data on a magnetic surface. The two basic types of floppies are the 5¼-inch disk and the 3½-inch disk.

HOW DISKS ARE ORGANIZED

Information is physically stored on a disk in concentric circles called tracks. Each track is divided into smaller areas called sectors. (See Figure 3-1.) Each sector, in turn, can store a fixed number of bytes. A sector is normally about 512 bytes.

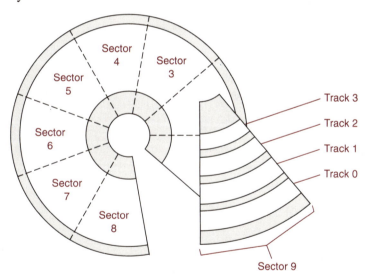

FIGURE 3-1. *Disk tracks and sectors.*

How many tracks and sectors a disk contains varies with the type of disk. Figure 3-2 shows the values for common types of floppy disks. The number of tracks and sectors on a hard disk varies with the manufacturer, the model, and the disk size.

Disk	Capacity (approx. bytes)	Sectors/Track	Tracks/Side
5¼-inch high-capacity	1.2 MB	15	80
5¼-inch double-sided	360 KB	9	40
3½-inch high-capacity	1.44 MB	18	80
3½-inch double-sided	720 KB	9	80

FIGURE 3-2. *Common types of floppy disks.*

Disk capacity depends on the number of tracks, sectors, and bytes available. The process of defining the tracks and sectors on the disk is called formatting.

You can use the Shell to find the capacity of any disk and to see how much of the space you have used.

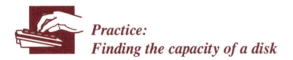

Practice:
Finding the capacity of a disk

1. Choose drive C from the drive list.
2. From the Options menu, choose Show Information. In addition to some other information, your screen (Figure 3-3) now tells you the volume name of the disk, the size of the disk, the amount of available space, and the number of files and directories on the disk.

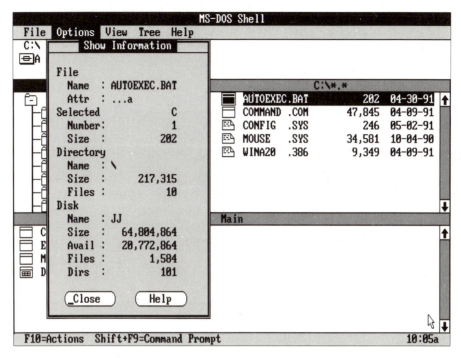

FIGURE 3-3. *Finding information about a disk.*

FILE MANAGEMENT ON A DISK

The DOS file management system views the disk as a collection of clusters. A cluster is a fixed number of bytes (or sectors) that can be addressed by the index on the disk. For most systems, a cluster is about 1024 or 2048 bytes (two or four sectors), depending on how the disk is formatted. A cluster is the smallest addressable unit on a DOS disk. A file, then, is stored as one or more clusters.

A directory listing might show a file as containing 3124 bytes. In reality, on the disk the file might be stored as two clusters and require 4096 bytes. The smallest file takes 2048 bytes. Figure 3-4 (on the following page) shows the number of bytes per cluster for common disk types.

DOS supports either one or two drives for floppy disks. If only a single drive is installed, it can be addressed as either A or B. If two drives are installed, one is A and the other is B.

Disk	Bytes/Cluster
5¼-inch (360 KB)	1024
5¼-inch (1.2 MB)	512
3½-inch (720 KB)	1024
3½-inch (1.4 MB)	512
PC/XT hard disk	4096
PC/AT hard disk	2048
(other hard disks can vary)	

FIGURE 3-4. *Cluster mapping for common disk types.*

A bootable disk is one from which you can load DOS. It can be a floppy disk or a hard disk. When you turn on the computer, the computer first checks the floppy-disk drives for a bootable disk. If none is found, the computer searches the hard disk.

At the very front (outer tracks) of every disk (whether you can boot from it or not) is a reserved area that contains a small boot program, the FAT (File Allocation Table), the directory, and the file area. If the disk is bootable, the first two files in the file area are the DOS files. The small boot program can find these DOS files only by their physical location. The directory area contains the root directory of the disk. For each file in the root, the directory entry contains the filename and extension, the date and time of the last edit, the file attributes (which designate the file as hidden, system, archive, or read-only), the file size, and the first cluster number of the file. The FAT is used to find the remaining clusters of the file.

If the disk is new, DOS places files on the disk so that they have contiguous (adjacent) clusters. As files are deleted, empty clusters appear where the deleted files were. As the disk fills, DOS stores new file clusters wherever it can find space. The clusters for any file are scattered at different locations on the disk. The FAT defines how the clusters for a particular file are linked.

From the user's perspective, however, as files are added, the files become fragmented, and the disk speed slows. Each time you use a file with scattered clusters, DOS has to spend a lot of time managing the disk access. To keep the disk speed fast, you should periodically use a defragmentation utility to physically reorder the disk so that the clusters for each file are adjacent.

PREPARING A DISK FOR USE

Before you can use either a hard disk or a floppy disk, the disk must be formatted, or prepared, for storing files.

Formatting a hard disk is a two-step process. Step 1, called a low-level format, is generally done by the manufacturer. Step 2 is part of installing DOS. If you are already using the DOS Shell, your hard disk is formatted, and you probably won't need to format it again unless the hard disk becomes defective. In fact, formatting the hard disk generally destroys all the information stored on it.

Formatting a floppy disk is a one-step process and can be done with the DOS Shell. Floppy disks that you purchase are seldom formatted, and so you must format them. You also should format old floppy disks when you can't read the data on them. Formatting destroys all data on the disk, but at least you might be able to reuse the disk. Formatting a disk is also useful when you intend to destroy data on the disk.

Practice:
Formatting a floppy disk

1. Move to the Program list area, and choose Disk Utilities if it is not already active.

2. Choose Format from the Disk Utilities program group.

3. The Format dialog box shows A as the drive to format. Choose OK or press Enter.

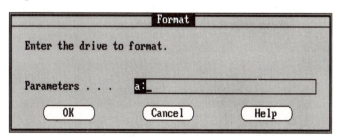

4. When prompted, place the disk in a drive and press Enter. The screen shows the progress of the formatting as a percentage of the disk formatted. The disk drive light stays on during formatting.

5. When the formatting is complete, you are asked for a volume label. (See "Naming a Disk," later in this chapter.) Enter a name that has no more than 11 characters, and then press Enter. If you don't want to label the disk, simply press Enter.

6. The screen shows information about the newly formatted disk. Press Y to format another disk; press N to end. For now, press N and then Enter.

7. Press any key to return to the Shell.

8. To return to the Main program group, choose Main or press Esc.

This formatting process creates a nonbootable disk that can store both data and programs.

NOTE: The type of drive determines the type of format. For example, if you place a 360-KB disk in a high-capacity 1.2-MB drive, the Shell tries (and probably fails) to format the disk to 1.2 MB. Always format disks in the appropriate drive.

After installing DOS 5, create a bootable floppy disk. If your hard disk fails, you can use this disk to restart your computer.

File Insurance

Formatting erases all contents of a disk. You can sometimes get files back by using the UNFORMAT command. (See "Recovering a Disk," later in this chapter.) Check disks before formatting to ensure that you are not destroying files you want to keep. To check a disk with the Shell, insert the disk and select the drive from the Shell's drive list.

The Quick Format disk utility erases the directory of a disk but leaves the data intact. You cannot use this command with a disk that has never been formatted.

You can get an error message when formatting a floppy disk. When this happens, discard the disk.

Chapter 3: Managing Disks

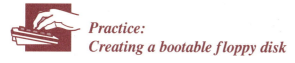

Practice:
Creating a bootable floppy disk

1. Move to the Program list area, and choose Command Prompt from the Main program group.

2. At the prompt, type:

   FORMAT *driveletter*: /S

   substituting for *driveletter* the name of the drive (A or B) in which you have inserted the floppy disk. Press Enter.

3. When the formatting is complete, type a volume name. At the prompt, type *EXIT* and press Enter to return to the Shell.

4. Copy the AUTOEXEC.BAT and the CONFIG.SYS files from the root directory of the hard drive to the formatted disk.

5. With the floppy disk in drive A, press Ctrl+Alt+Del to reboot your computer and thus ensure that you have created a bootable disk.

6. Label the disk BOOT DISK DOS VERSION 5.00.

If you have special formatting requirements, use the DOS FORMAT command to format the floppy disk for these requirements. Information on this command is found in Chapter 6 and in your DOS manual.

NAMING A DISK

The name you assign to a disk is called the volume name. The name can have as many as 11 characters, and it has no extension. Use names that suggest the contents of the disk. You can change the volume name of a disk; doing so does not alter the contents.

Practice:
Changing a volume name

1. Move to the Program list area, and choose Command Prompt from the Main program group.

2. Switch to the drive that contains the disk you want to rename.

3. Type *LABEL* at the prompt.

4. The screen shows the current volume name. Type the new name and press Enter.

5. Type *EXIT* and press Enter to return to the Shell.

When you choose Show Information from the Options menu, the volume name of the selected drive appears in the disk section of the dialog box.

COPYING A FLOPPY DISK

When you copy a floppy disk, the entire contents of the disk are duplicated on another disk. The source disk contains the information you want to copy. The destination disk receives a copy of the contents of the source disk.

The two floppy disks must be the same size and the same type. You can copy a 360-KB disk to another 360-KB disk, but you can't copy a 360-KB disk to a 1.2-MB disk.

All preexisting contents of the destination disk are destroyed and cannot be recovered. Be sure the destination disk contains nothing you want to keep. You need not format the destination disk; the copy operation formats it.

Copying a boot disk creates a destination boot disk. System files and hidden files are copied. Be sure that the source disk is write-protected before you make a copy.

Practice:
Copying a floppy disk

1. Move to the Program list area, and choose Disk Utilities.

2. Choose Disk Copy from the Disk Utilities program group.

3. In the Disk Copy dialog box, enter the source drive (*A:*) and the destination drive (*B:*).

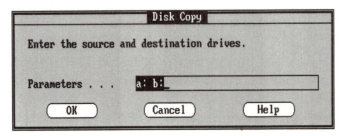

4. Choose OK or press Enter.

5. Follow the prompts, and insert the disk as requested.

6. When the copy is complete, press Y to copy another disk or N to end the operation.

7. Press any key to return to the Shell.

NOTE: You can copy one floppy disk to another using a single drive. For example, to copy a low-density disk (360 KB) with a single low-capacity drive B, type B: B: *in the Disk Copy dialog box. DOS prompts you when you need to change floppy disks.*

Backing Up Program Disks

When you install a new program, first copy the manufacturer's master disks, and then use the copies to install the program. Keep the master disks write-protected. Some programs write data to the installation disks, and you can't install them from a write-protected disk. In this case, copy the disk, and then install from the copy that isn't write-protected.

COMPARING DISKS

To ensure that you indeed have an exact copy of a disk, you need to compare the source disk and the destination disk. The Shell does not have a Compare command, but you can compare disks from within the Shell by using the DOS COMP command.

Practice:
Comparing disks

1. Be sure both disks are write-protected.

2. Place one disk in drive A and the other in drive B.

3. From the File menu, choose Run.

4. In the Run dialog box, type:

   COMP

   and press Enter or choose OK.

 NOTE: You can compare one disk with another disk using a single drive. For example, to use a low-capacity B drive to compare two low-density disks (360 KB), type DISKCOMP B: B: *in the dialog box. DOS prompts you when you need to change floppy disks.*

RECOVERING A DISK

If you format a disk and then realize you did so by mistake, you can sometimes recover the data with the UNFORMAT command.

1. Place the disk you want to recover in drive A.
2. From the File menu, choose Run.
3. In the dialog box, type:

   UNFORMAT A:

   and press Enter or choose OK. The screen displays a warning.
4. Press Y.

The disk is now rebuilt to its preformat condition.

The DOS UNFORMAT command must be used immediately after the mistaken FORMAT command. If the disk was formatted using other formatting programs, or if the files were lost or damaged for other reasons, you cannot recover the files.

 NOTE: The UNFORMAT command cannot always restore all files lost as a result of formatting. For example, if the formatting was unconditional (using the /u parameter), no files can be restored.

DISK MANAGEMENT TIPS

- Treat your disks as software resources, not as hardware. Disks are valuable because of the information they contain, but you should handle even blank disks with care. Poor handling can make a disk less reliable for data storage in the future.

- Never touch the magnetic surface of a disk. Oil from your fingers can transfer to the disk surface, attracting dust.

- Keep 5¼-inch disks in their paper jackets when they aren't in the drive, to protect the read/write access opening. When mailing disks, be sure to use mailers designed specifically for disks.

- Disks store information as magnetic patterns, so you need to keep disks away from magnetic or electromagnetic fields that could destroy the patterns. Don't put disks near a telephone, a desk lamp (or a lamp base), computer power supplies, or speakers.

- Keep food, drinks, and cigarettes away from disks. Even cigarette smoke is dangerous for disks.

- Don't fold or staple disks or use paper clips with them.

- Avoid stacking disks or placing objects on top of them. Store them vertically.

- Don't try to modify a disk to make it work for another format.

- Label a disk immediately after storing information on it. Doing so helps minimize unintentional deletions or accidental formatting.

- When writing on disk labels, avoid using pencils or ballpoint pens. Pens can crease the magnetic surface, and pencils can damage the surface. Use a felt-tip pen only.

- Protect disks from excessive cold, heat, or humidity.

- Use caution in formatting disks. Formatting a hard disk or a floppy disk causes the loss of data on the disk, although some level of recovery is possible. The safest rule is never to use the Shell to format a hard disk.

- To speed disk operation, use a defragmentation program (such as PC Tools) periodically to reorder the clusters for each file so that they are sequential on the hard disk.

- The X-ray machines used in airport security systems are not likely to harm disks, but the magnetic fields generated by the machines will. Passing disks around an X-ray machine might do even more damage than letting them go through on the conveyor belt; passing disks around a machine can place them close to the machine's magnetic field. Carrying disks in suitcases can risk exposing them to electromagnetic scanners. In short, leave master disks at home and take only copies when you travel on airplanes.

Chapter 4

Managing Directories

A typical hard disk might contain more than 2000 files. You can organize these files into directories and subdirectories, creating a personalized structure that helps you find and use your files more efficiently.

INTRODUCTION TO USING DIRECTORIES

A directory is actually an index to a collection of files. DOS uses this index to locate files. For each file in the directory, the index contains the filename, the size of the file, a date and time stamp that shows when the file was created or last changed, and the file attributes. The index also contains the location of the first cluster of the file.

All disks have at least one directory—the root directory—which is created when the disk is formatted. The root directory is designated with a backslash (\).

The root directory is stored in a fixed amount of physical space at the beginning of the disk. When this physical space is used up, you cannot put more files in the root directory unless you make more space by deleting files.

You can, and should, create more directories on the disk to improve file management. Directory organization is much like a tree with branches. In fact, the first directory is called the root, and the display is called a Directory Tree. Directories can have other directories within them to any level. This kind of directory organization is referred to as a hierarchical structure.

Now let's explore the directories on your disk. Start the DOS Shell, and examine the Directory Tree (Figure 4-1). At the top of the list is C:\, which is the root directory. A vertical line descends from this, which represents the trunk of the tree. Branching off this line are a number of other directories: DOS, OLD_DOS.1, and WP. You might have similar (and additional) directories on your disk. These are subdirectories of the root directory. A subdirectory is a directory within another directory. A parent is the directory in which you place a subdirectory. In this example, the root directory is the parent, and the subdirectories are the children.

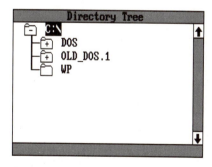

FIGURE 4-1. *The Shell Directory Tree.*

Some directories have a plus (+) next to their name, which indicates that the directory has another directory or directories under it. Click the plus (+) or select the directory and press a plus (+) to see the subdirectories. To hide them, click the minus (–) next to the parent directory name or select the directory and press a minus (–).

DOS creates a file in the parent for each child directory. This file won't show up in the Shell's File list, but it's still there, takes space, and counts as a file entry in the parent directory. When counting entries in the root directory, you must count both normal files and a directory entry for each first-level branch in the Directory Tree that is displayed. When the root directory is full, you get an out-of-space message from DOS, even if the disk actually contains more space.

In reality, all directories except the root are subdirectories, but in this book we will call them directories and refer to them as subdirectories only when referencing a relationship. The directory that you are using at a given time is called the current directory.

Each directory is private in the sense that it cannot share information with other directories. Two files can have the same name on the disk, as long as they are in different directories. Two directories can have the same name, as long as they have different parents.

When you specify a file for a program, you must specify its location in the directory structure in order to find it. To see how this works, let's execute a program.

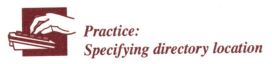

Practice:
Specifying directory location

1. From the File menu, choose Run.

2. At the Command Line prompt, type:

   C:\DOS\CHKDSK.EXE

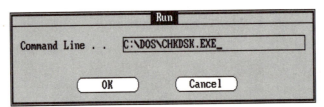

Chapter 4: Managing Directories

3. Choose OK or press Enter.

4. Press any key to return to the Shell.

The C:\DOS\ designator is called the pathname. You typed the drive name for the program file, the route to the file (the path), and the filename. The directory and the filename are separated by a backslash (\).

Now do the above practice again, but omit *C:\DOS* from the line you type. Simply type *CHKDSK.EXE*.

If your system is set up properly, this second method will work just as well as the first. The AUTOEXEC.BAT file in the root directory of the disk is read each time you boot the computer. It uses the PATH command of DOS to define a series of paths that enable the Shell to find the CHKDSK program.

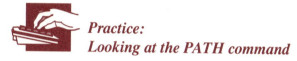

Practice:
Looking at the PATH command

1. Move to the Program list area, and choose the Editor from the Main program group.

2. Type *AUTOEXEC.BAT* in the File to Edit dialog box.

3. Choose OK or press Enter.

4. Notice that the PATH command (seen in Figure 4-2, on the following page) specifies the C:\DOS directory as an alternate directory. Press Alt+F and then X to return to the Shell.

The PATH command tells DOS where to look for program files (files with .EXE, .COM, and .BAT extensions), not data files. Because the Editor regards the AUTOEXEC.BAT file as a text file, the Editor cannot use the PATH command to find the file. Check to be sure that the root directory is selected before you load this file.

53

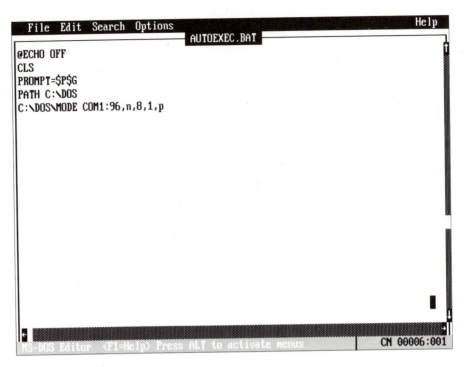

FIGURE 4-2. *The default AUTOEXEC.BAT file.*

NAMING DIRECTORIES

You can devise whatever names you like for directories (except for the root directory). The directory name can be from one to eight characters. Like a filename, it can also have an extension of one to three characters, separated from the name with a period, but an extension is not required. For the extension, you can use letters, numbers, and any of the following characters:

   ' ~ ! @ # $ % ^ & ( ) _ - { }

Some directory listings include a period (.) or double period (..).

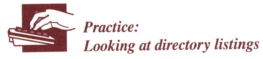

Practice:
Looking at directory listings

1. From the Directory Tree, select the DOS directory.

2. From the File menu, choose Run.

3. At the Command Line prompt, type:

   DIR/W/P

4. Choose OK or press Enter. The screen shows a directory listing something like the following:

```
Volume in drive C is JJ
Volume Serial Number is 1688-3C92
Directory of C:\DOS

[.]              [..]             EGA.SYS          FORMAT.COM       CLOCK.SYS
NLSFUNC.EXE      COUNTRY.SYS      DISPLAY.SYS      EGA.CPI          DRIVER33.SYS
HIMEM.SYS        KEYB.COM         KEYBOARD.SYS     MODE.COM         KEYB33.COM
KEYBRD33.SYS     MODE33.COM       SETVER.EXE       ANSI.SYS         VDISK.SYS
DEBUG.EXE        DOSKEY.COM       EDLIN.EXE        EMM386.EXE       FASTOPEN.EXE
FDISK.EXE        MEM.EXE          MIRROR.COM       RAMDRIVE.SYS     SHARE.EXE
SMARTDRV.SYS     SYS.COM          UNDELETE.EXE     UNFORMAT.COM     XCOPY.EXE
DOSSHELL.VID     LINK.EXE         DOSSHELL.COM     DOSSHELL.EXE     DOSSHELL.GRB
DOSSWAP.EXE      PACKING.LST      PRINT.EXE        DOSHELP.HLP      BASIC.COM
BASICA.COM       BASICA.EXE       DOSSHELL.HLP     HELP.EXE         RECOVER.EXE
SETCLOCK.COM     INTEREST.BAS     EDIT.HLP         QBASIC.HLP       EDIT.COM
WHERE.EXE        MSHERC.COM       QBASIC.EXE       GORILLA.BAS      MONEY.BAS
NIBBLES.BAS      REMLINE.BAS      APPEND.EXE       ATTRIB.EXE       BACKUP.EXE
CHKDSK.EXE       COMP.EXE         DISKCOMP.COM     DISKCOPY.COM     FC.EXE
FIND.EXE         LABEL.EXE        MORE.COM         RESTORE.EXE      SORT.EXE
4201.CPI         4208.CPI         5202.CPI         ASSIGN.COM       DRIVER.SYS
GRAFTABL.COM     GRAPHICS.COM     GRAPHICS.PRO     JOIN.EXE         LCD.CPI
PRINTER.SYS      EXE2BIN.EXE      REPLACE.EXE      TREE.COM         SUBST.EXE
LOADFIX.COM      README.TXT       APPNOTES.TXT     EXPAND.EXE       DELOLDOS.EXE
Press any key to continue . . .
```

Notice the period and double period at the top of the list. The period is an abbreviation for the current directory; the double period is an abbreviation for the parent directory.

5. Press any key to see the rest of the listing.

6. Press any key to return to the Shell.

THE INITIAL DIRECTORY DISPLAY

When you start the Shell, the boot disk drive (C) is displayed at the top of the drive list. The Directory Tree shows a single directory level; that is, you can see the subdirectories of the root directory (see Figure 4-1, on page 51), but no farther. The full path for the current directory is displayed below the menu bar and at the top of the File list area. The File list area shows the files in the currently selected directory.

CREATING NEW DIRECTORIES

You can customize your disk to meet specific needs and to organize files efficiently by creating multiple directories.

Practice:
Creating a new directory

1. From the Directory Tree, select the DOS directory.
2. Choose the File menu, and then choose Create Directory.
3. Type *TEST* as the new directory name.

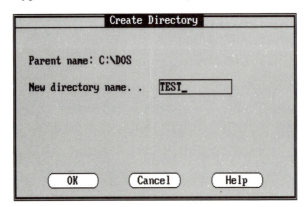

4. Press Enter or choose OK.

The Directory Tree now shows the new directory TEST (Figure 4-3).

Chapter 4: Managing Directories

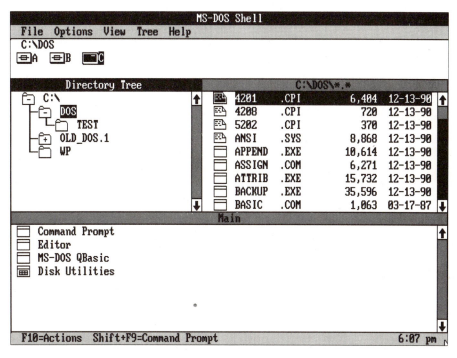

FIGURE 4-3. *The new directory TEST.*

RENAMING DIRECTORIES

To ensure that disk organization accurately reflects content, you occasionally need to rename a directory.

Practice:
Renaming a directory

1. From the Directory Tree, select the new TEST directory.
2. Choose the File menu, and then choose Rename.
3. Type *TEMP* as the new directory name.

57

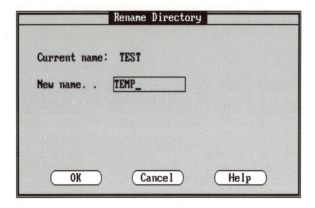

4. Press Enter or choose OK. The Directory Tree shows the updated directory name TEMP.

You can't name or rename a directory with a name that already appears in the current directory. If you get an error message when you try to rename, check to see whether a file or a directory already exists under that name in the parent directory.

DELETING DIRECTORIES

When you no longer use a directory, you can delete it. Before you can delete a directory, however, you must delete any files it contains. To try the practice below, copy several files to the TEMP directory you just created. (Chapter 2 explains how to copy files; be sure to copy them rather than moving them.)

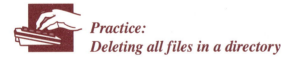

Practice:
Deleting all files in a directory

1. From the Directory Tree, select the TEMP directory.
2. Tab to the File list area.
3. Choose the File menu, and then choose Select All.
4. Press Del or, from the File menu, choose Delete.
5. Choose OK or press Enter in the Delete File dialog box.
6. Choose Yes or press Enter in each Delete File Confirmation dialog box as it appears.

 *Practice:*
Deleting a directory

1. From the Directory Tree, select the TEMP directory.
2. Choose the File menu.
3. Choose Delete or press Del.
4. Choose Yes in the Delete Directory Confirmation box.

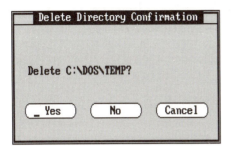

If you think you have deleted all the files, but you are still unable to delete the directory, be sure that (1) you are in the parent directory of the directory you want to delete and (2) the directory you are deleting has no subdirectories or hidden files.

ORGANIZING DIRECTORIES

When you install DOS, a DOS directory is created as a subdirectory of the root directory, and most DOS files are placed here. Keep this directory for DOS files only so that updating to future versions of DOS will be easier.

Add a TEMP directory as a subdirectory of the root directory (if you don't already have one) for temporary files created by programs. You should also make a directory for each application—for example, your word processing program should have its own directory. Again, updating to future versions will be easier.

Now that you know something about directories, you can use the entire pathname in referencing a directory. For example, instead of referring to the DOS subdirectory of the root directory, you can call it \DOS.

Many users find it helpful to add a directory named OLD. If you run across a strange file and wonder whether you need it, move it to the OLD directory. If everything continues to work well for a few months, chances are the file is not important and can be deleted. If some program tries to look for the file, however, move it back where it came from.

 CAUTION: If your system is part of a network, the network administrator often defines some rules for directories on the computers in the network. Check with the network administrator before you get too creative.

TIPS FOR USING DIRECTORIES

- Whenever possible, try to work with a single directory level below the root. Using one level whenever you can minimizes typing and speeds disk access. Some programs can install themselves with multiple levels. Don't try to reorganize these.
- DOS 5 installs its files in a \DOS directory. Don't put anything else in that directory.
- Create a \BAT directory for batch files. (See Chapter 9.)
- Keep utilities in their own directories. For example, you might keep common utilities in a \UTIL directory. Keep commercial utilities in their own directories, with names such as \NORTON or \PCTOOLS. Commercial utilities, in general, work faster if they are started from a first-level directory rather than as subdirectories of a \UTIL directory.
- Create a \TEMP directory for temporary files. Some programs use this directory for their temporary files if it exists. Keep it empty.
- Create an \OLD directory for miscellaneous files that you don't want to delete quite yet.
- Keep applications in their own directories. For example, keep Microsoft Word in an \MW or a \WORD directory. Updating to future versions will be easier, and making backups is simpler. You need not back up program directories unless they are changed.

- Define data directories in such a way that backup work is simplified. For example, keep all files on a related project together in a directory (word processing, spreadsheets, and database files for a single project).

- Create batch files to start programs (as discussed in Chapter 9), keeping these files in the \BAT directory. The PATH command of the AUTOEXEC.BAT file should set a default path to include \BAT, \UTIL (and other utility directories), and program directories used frequently.

- Minimize the number of files kept in the root directories. Unlike other directories, root directories are stored in a fixed amount of physical space. If you store too many files in the root directory, you will get an out-of-disk-space message. A subdirectory entry counts as a file.

- Name directories in a way that logically identifies the contents.

- Use a directory structure that is meaningful in terms of how you use the disk.

- Avoid putting more than about 100 files in any directory. DOS slows down dramatically if too many files are in a directory.

- Use short directory names without extensions; long filenames involve more typing. DOS limits a pathname to 64 characters.

Chapter 5

Running Applications

Using the Shell, you can run an application by clicking on its name. When the application terminates, control is returned to the Shell. You can also run multiple programs simultaneously.

STARTING AN APPLICATION

You can start an application from the Program list area, from the File list, from the File menu, or from the command prompt. When you use the mouse, double-click on the application name. When you use the keyboard, select or type the name and press Enter.

From the Program List Area

When you install the Shell, the Program list area contains two program groups: Main and Disk Utilities. The Main program group includes Command Prompt, the Editor, and MS-DOS QBasic (Figure 5-1).

```
┌─────────────────────────── Main ───────────────────────────┐
│ 🗎 Command Prompt                                         ↑│
│ 🗎 Editor                                                  │
│ 🗎 MS-DOS QBasic                                           │
│ 📰 Disk Utilities                                          │
│                                                            │
│                                                            │
│                                                           ↓│
└────────────────────────────────────────────────────────────┘
```

FIGURE 5-1. *The Main program group.*

Disk Utilities is a program group contained in the Main group. It includes Disk Copy, Backup Fixed Disk, Restore Fixed Disk, Quick Format, Format, and Undelete (Figure 5-2).

```
┌─────────────────────── Disk Utilities ─────────────────────┐
│ 📰 Main                                                   ↑│
│ 🗎 Disk Copy                                               │
│ 🗎 Backup Fixed Disk                                       │
│ 🗎 Restore Fixed Disk                                      │
│ 🗎 Quick Format                                            │
│ 🗎 Format                                                  │
│ 🗎 Undelete                                                │
│                                                           ↓│
└────────────────────────────────────────────────────────────┘
```

FIGURE 5-2. *Programs in Disk Utilities.*

Practice:
Starting the Editor from the Main program group

1. Move to the Program list area.
2. Choose the Main program group if it is not already active.
3. Choose the Editor.
4. In the File to Edit dialog box, choose OK or press Enter.
5. When the Welcome dialog box appears, press Esc to clear the screen. You can now create a file with the Editor. To return to the Shell, choose the File menu, and then choose Exit.

For information on how to use the Editor, see Chapter 8.

NOTE: When you start a program from the Main group, the Shell remembers and highlights that program the next time you select the Main group.

From the File List

You can start programs from executable files on the File list or from data files on the File list. Executable files have the extension .EXE or .COM. The Editor is an executable file. Let's run it again—this time from the File list.

 *Practice:*
Starting the Editor from the File list

1. From the Directory Tree, select the DOS directory.
2. Choose EDIT.COM from the File list.
3. When the Welcome dialog box appears, press Esc to clear the screen.
4. To return to the Shell, choose the File menu, and then choose Exit. Press any key when you are prompted to do so.

Before you can start an application program from a data file, you must associate the file with the program. For practice, let's associate all files that have a .DOC extension with your word processor and then run the word processor by choosing a .DOC file.

Chapter 5: Running Applications

 Practice:
Associating files and starting a program from a data file

1. Select the directory that contains your word processing files.

2. From the File list, select a file that has the .DOC extension.

3. From the File menu, choose Associate.

4. In the Associate File dialog box, type the name of your word processing program.

5. Press Enter or choose OK. All files that have the .DOC extension are now associated with your word processor.

6. Choose a file with the .DOC extension. The file is displayed from within your word processing program and can be edited.

7. To return to the Shell, quit the word processor.

 Starting an application from a data file is handy for accessing programs you use frequently. For example, it's convenient to access your word processor from any .DOC file, the Editor from any .TXT file, and QBasic from any .BAS file.

From the File Menu

Starting an application with the Run command from the File menu is sometimes the fastest way to access a program. This method is also useful if you need to supply startup options. Once again, let's start the Editor.

 Practice:
Starting the Editor from the File menu

1. From the File menu, choose Run.

2. In the Run dialog box, type:

   EDIT.COM

3. Choose OK or press Enter. Press Esc to clear the screen.

4. To return to the Shell, choose the File menu, and then choose Exit. Press any key when you are prompted to do so.

67

From the Command Prompt

Although starting an application from the command prompt can seem to be the most difficult method, it is useful to know this technique. (For details on using the command prompt, see Chapter 6.)

Practice:
Starting the Editor from the command prompt

1. Move to the Program list area.
2. Choose the Main program group if it is not already active.
3. Choose Command Prompt from the Main program group.
4. At the DOS command prompt (C:\>), type:

   EDIT.COM

   and press Enter. Press Esc to clear the screen.
5. To return to the Shell, choose the File menu, and then choose Exit.
   At the DOS command prompt, type *EXIT* and press Enter.

ADDING PROGRAMS TO THE MAIN GROUP

Adding programs to the Main program group is one way of customizing the Shell to fit your own needs. You can add a program item or a program group. You use the commands on the File menu to add an item or a group. Select the Main group, and then choose the File menu (Figure 5-3). Notice that the list of choices is different from the list that is available when the File list is selected.

FIGURE 5-3. *The File menu.*

Program Items

One useful addition to the Main program group is your word processor. If you add it as a program item, you can run it from the Main group.

Practice:
Adding a word processor as a program item

1. Move to the Program list area.

2. Choose the Main program group if it is not already active.

3. From the File menu, choose New.

4. In the New Program Object dialog box, be sure that Program Item is selected, and then choose OK or press Enter.

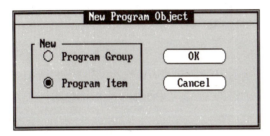

5. In the Add Program dialog box, type the name of the program in the Program Title field. Tab to the Commands field, and type the command you use to start the program.

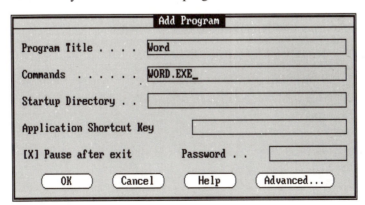

The remaining fields in the Add Program dialog box are optional. The only fields you must complete are the Program Title field and the Commands field.

6. Choose OK or press Enter.
7. To run the program item you have added, double-click on it, or select it and press Enter. To return to the Shell from the program, quit the program.

You can add other information to the Commands field and complete the optional fields to gain even greater control over starting application programs. To see some of the possibilities, select the Editor. Now choose Properties from the File menu. Figure 5-4 shows the Program Item Properties dialog box as it appears on your screen.

```
┌─────────────────Program Item Properties─────────────────┐
│ Program Title  . . . . [Editor_                       ] │
│ Commands  . . . . . .  [EDIT %1                       ] │
│ Startup Directory . .  [                              ] │
│ Application Shortcut Key  [                           ] │
│ [ ] Pause after exit      Password . . [              ] │
│        ( OK )   ( Cancel )   ( Help )  ( Advanced... )  │
└─────────────────────────────────────────────────────────┘
```

FIGURE 5-4. *The Program Item Properties dialog box.*

Notice that in the Commands field, the EDIT command is followed by the notation %1. This notation is called a parameter. In this case, %1 represents any filename you want to see when you run the Editor. You can have as many as 10 parameters. (See Chapters 6 and 7 for more information on parameters and their use.)

In Figure 5-4, the Startup Directory field is blank. You can use this field to specify a directory other than the one in which the program normally resides.

Also blank in Figure 5-4 is the Application Shortcut Key field. In this field, you can specify keyboard shortcuts—similar to the key combinations that you can use for menu items. The shortcut must be Shift, Alt, or Ctrl, combined with another key.

The Password field is also blank. You can use this field to restrict access to a program only to those who know the password. The password can be from 1 to 20 characters, including spaces. To delete a password, choose Properties from the File menu, and then select the Password field. Press Backspace to delete the password.

When you run an application program from the Shell and then return to the Shell, you might see the following message on the screen:

```
Press any key to return to MS-DOS Shell....
```

You can control the display of this message with the check box that precedes the line *Pause after exit* in the Program Item Properties dialog box.

Notice that the Advanced command button in this dialog box contains an ellipsis, indicating that another dialog box is available. Figure 5-5 shows this second dialog box as it exists for the Editor. Your DOS manual contains detailed information on using the Advanced dialog box.

FIGURE 5-5. *The Advanced dialog box.*

Program Groups

When you install the Shell, you have two program groups: Main and Disk Utilities. But you can create other groups. For example, you might want a group named Financial that includes a spreadsheet program, a database management program, and any other programs you normally use when producing financial reports or formulating budgets. You then can run these programs from the program items in the program group.

NOTE: Programs can be in more than one group. This doesn't mean that you have multiple copies of the program on disk. It does mean that you can access programs in multiple ways, which can save you time and make it easier to find and use your files.

Practice:
Adding a Financial program group

1. Move to the Program list area.

2. Choose the Main program group if it is not already active.

3. From the File menu, choose New.

4. In the New Program Object dialog box, select Program Group, and then choose OK or press Enter.

5. In the Add Group dialog box, type *FINANCIAL*, the program group title. Adding Help text or a password is optional.

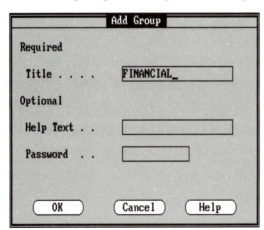

6. Choose OK or press Enter.

Chapter 5: Running Applications

Financial appears in the Program list area as a program group. You can now add program items to this group, as you did earlier with the Main group.

NOTE: Program groups are organized in a hierarchical structure similar to the Directory Tree. The Main program group is like the root directory, and other program groups are like subdirectories. You can put program groups inside program groups, just as you can put subdirectories inside subdirectories. And you can always return to the Main program group simply by pressing Esc.

Ordering the Program List

If you have a number of items on your Program list, you can reorder them so that those most frequently used, for example, appear first.

Practice:
Reordering program items

1. In the Program list area, select the program item.
2. From the File menu, choose Reorder.
3. Double-click on the line under the new location, or move the cursor to it and press Enter.

Deleting Program Items and Groups

When you delete a program from the Program list area, you are not deleting it from the disk; you are simply deleting it from the Program list. You use the same procedure to delete program items or program groups.

Practice:
Deleting a program item

1. In the Program list area, select the program item to be deleted.
2. From the File menu, choose Delete, or press Del.

RUNNING MULTIPLE PROGRAMS SIMULTANEOUSLY

When you install the Shell, the Task Swapper is not enabled. As you now know, your initial screen looks like the one shown in Figure 5-6.

The Task Swapper is the tool that you use to run more than one program at a time. For example, you can run both the Editor and MS-DOS QBasic simultaneously.

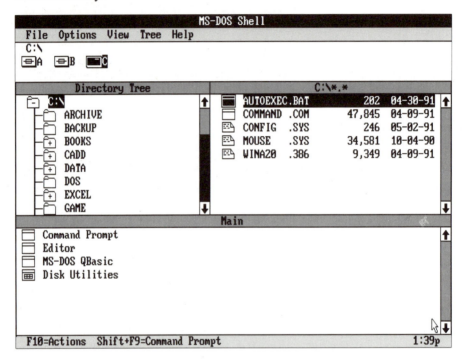

FIGURE 5-6. *The Shell screen with the Task Swapper disabled.*

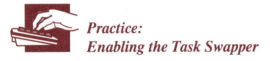

Practice:
Enabling the Task Swapper

1. From the Options menu, choose Enable Task Swapper.
2. Now the Task Swapper is enabled, and your screen looks something like the one shown in Figure 5-7 (on the next page).

Chapter 5: Running Applications

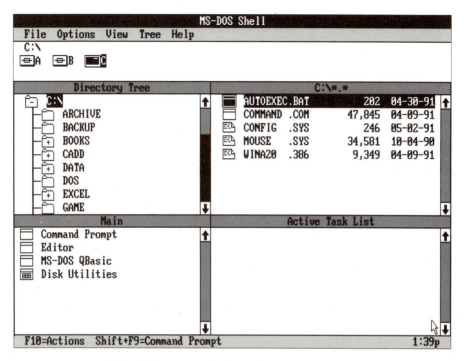

FIGURE 5-7. *The Shell screen with the Task Swapper enabled.*

The portion of the screen that displays the names of running programs is the Active Task List. When program names appear here, you can switch to the programs from the Active Task List in the same way you start them from the Program list area.

Let's start a couple of programs to see how the Task Swapper works.

Practice:
Running two programs simultaneously

1. With the Task Swapper enabled, start the Editor from the Main program group in the Program list area.

2. In the File to Edit dialog box, type:

   TEXT.TXT

3. Choose OK or press Enter.

4. You can now edit this file with the Editor. To return to the Shell, press Alt+Tab or Ctrl+Esc—either choice will get you there. The Editor now appears in the Active Task List.

5. Start MS-DOS QBasic from the Main program group in the Program list area.

6. In the MS-DOS QBasic File dialog box, type:

   TEST.BAS

7. Choose OK or press Enter.

8. To return to the Shell from MS-DOS QBasic, press Alt+Tab or Ctrl+Esc. The Active Task List now shows two running programs: the Editor and MS-DOS QBasic.

NOTE: The number of programs you can add to the Active Task List depends on the memory and disk space of your computer system. The Shell displays a message if it runs out of space.

To return to a program that is on the Active Task List, simply double-click on it, or select it and press Enter.

If the Shell screen is displayed, press Alt+Tab to return to the program you used most recently. Pressing Alt+Tab repeatedly cycles through the Shell and all the programs that are running.

To remove a program from the Active Task List, switch to the program and then quit it as you normally would (not by pressing Alt+Tab or Ctrl+Esc). Terminating the program returns you to the Shell and removes the program from the Active Task List. You cannot exit the Shell while any programs remain in the Active Task List. You must first terminate all running programs.

If a program fails unexpectedly, press Alt+Tab to return to the Shell. Then close each running program, quit the Shell, and reboot the computer.

TIPS FOR RUNNING APPLICATIONS

- Keep frequently used programs on the Program list, the place from which it is easiest to start programs.

- Organize program groups logically, placing frequently used items in the same group.

- Study the groups and items installed with DOS for clues about the best way to set up your program items and program groups.

- Use the Run command on the File menu as the fastest way to start a program that is not on the Program list or the File list.

Chapter 6

At the Command Prompt

In this chapter, you learn how to leave the Shell and use the DOS command prompt (C:\>). At the command prompt, you give instructions directly to the operating system, rather than issuing them via the Shell.

Why and under what circumstances should you use the command prompt rather than the Shell?

- Certain commands, such as those that set your system date and time, are available only at the command prompt.
- The Shell uses memory. Some applications need a lot of memory and thus run more efficiently when executed from DOS rather than from within the Shell.
- DOS has many utilities. Sometimes it is easier to use them directly from the command prompt.
- If you are using many programs, starting them from the command prompt can be easier than locating them in the Shell.

You can add most of the programs in this chapter to the Shell. If one is particularly valuable or if you use it frequently, add it to the Shell Program list.

THE DOS COMMAND PROMPT

DOS displays the command prompt when the operating system is waiting for a command. The command prompt is your interface with the computer if you aren't using the Shell. This chapter assumes that DOS is installed on drive C, your hard-disk drive. Instructions to type something "at the prompt" refer to C:\>, which is also often called the C prompt.

USING THE COMMAND PROMPT

To access the command prompt from the Shell without removing the Shell from memory, choose Command Prompt from the Main program group in the Program list area or press Shift+F9. The Shell is still in memory, but you are now temporarily interfaced directly with DOS, and your screen shows the command prompt C:\>.

To access the command prompt from the Shell and remove the Shell from memory, press either F3 or Alt+F4 or choose Exit from the File menu.

To return to the Shell when it is still in memory, type *EXIT* at the command prompt and press Enter; if the Shell is not in memory, reload it by typing *DOSSHELL* instead.

For all commands entered at the command prompt, you can use either uppercase or lowercase letters. DOS is not sensitive to letter case.

Help

If you are a new user of DOS, one of the most important commands is HELP. To get a listing of all DOS commands and a brief description of each, simply type *HELP* at the command prompt. The listing covers several screens; to see the next screen, press any key.

To get information on a specific command, type *HELP* and the command at the prompt. For example, to get help with the CD (Change Directories) command, type:

```
HELP CD
```

at the prompt and press Enter. Figure 6-1 shows the information that now appears on your screen.

```
C:\>HELP CD
Displays the name of or changes the current directory.

CHDIR [drive:][path]
CHDIR[..]
CD [drive:][path]
CD[..]

  ..   Specifies that you want to change to the parent directory.

Type CD drive: to display the current directory in the specified drive.
Type CD without parameters to display the current drive and directory.

C:\>
```

FIGURE 6-1. *Help information about the CD command.*

Date and Time

When you are in the Shell, the current time is displayed in the lower right corner of your screen; the current date is not displayed.

To see or change the current date, type:

DATE

at the command prompt and press Enter. Your screen shows the current date as determined by your system and prompts you to enter a new date. If the date shown on the screen is correct, simply press Enter. To change the date, type the current date in the format shown in the prompt and then press Enter.

To see or change the current time, type:

TIME

at the command prompt and press Enter. Your screen shows the current time as determined by your system and prompts you to enter a new time. If the time shown is correct, simply press Enter. To change the time, type the current time in the format shown in the prompt and then press Enter.

Changing Drives

The C prompt indicates that drive C is the current drive. To access another drive, you must change to it. Be sure that a disk is in place if you are switching to a floppy-disk drive.

Practice:
Changing to drive A

1. At the prompt, type:

    A:

2. Now press Enter. Your screen shows the following:

    A:\>

3. To change back to drive C, type:

    C:

    and press Enter.

The DIR Command

DIR is a program that displays the contents of the current directory. The DIR program is internal to DOS; that is, you won't find it listed in the DOS directory, but it is built into DOS. To see a list of files and directories in the root directory, type:

    DIR

at the prompt and press Enter.

If the list is long, it scrolls off the screen. To stop the scrolling, press Ctrl+S or the Pause key. To resume scrolling, press any key. A better way to control the display is to type the following at the prompt:

    DIR/P

and press Enter. Now the program pauses after filling each screen. To see the next screenful of listings, press any key. (The following section explains the /p part of this command.)

The word <DIR> to the right of a filename indicates a subdirectory of the root directory. Hidden files and system files are not included. Listings of subdirectories include the date and time of their creation or most recent modification. Listings of files include their size and the date and time of their creation or most recent modification. Last on the list are the number of files in the current directory, the number of bytes used by the files in that directory, and the number of bytes available on the disk.

You can also get information about a specific file. For example, to see only the COMMAND.COM file, type:

    DIR COMMAND.COM

at the prompt and press Enter.

Parameters

In the command DIR/p, the /p is a parameter (also called an argument, an option, or a switch). A parameter indicates more specifically what the program is to do.

Another useful parameter is /w. At the prompt, type:

    DIR/W

and press Enter. Notice that you get less information on each file but that the filenames are arranged in columns.

Here are some other parameters that are frequently used with the DIR command:

DIR /a:-d	Displays only files in the current directory
DIR /a:s	Displays only system files in the current directory
DIR /a:d	Displays only subdirectories in the current directory
DIR /a:h	Displays only hidden files in the current directory
DIR /a:a	Displays files in the current directory that have been changed since the last backup
DIR /a:r	Displays read-only files in the current directory
DIR /o:n	Displays all files and directories in alphabetic order by name
DIR /o:d	Displays all files and directories in order by date and time, the earliest first
DIR /o:e	Displays files and directories in alphabetic order by filename extension
DIR /o:s	Displays files and directories in order by size, the smallest first
DIR /o:g	Displays files and directories, with the directories listed first

Many of the parameters listed here work in an opposite fashion if you place a hyphen before the last letter. For example, DIR /a:-s displays all files except system files, and DIR /o:-n lists the directories and files in reverse alphabetic order by name.

You can also combine parameters, and you can use directory paths and wildcards in the specification to display only a certain group of files. For example, the following command displays all .DOC files of the WP directory in name order:

```
DIR C:\WP\*.DOC /O:N
```

CHECKING THE DISK

Periodically, you should check your hard disk, using a DOS program called CHKDSK, which is run from the command prompt.

 CAUTION: Always remove the Shell from memory before you run CHKDSK from the command prompt. Running CHKDSK with the Shell in memory interferes with other programs.

To run CHKDSK, type:

CHKDSK

at the prompt and press Enter.

Figure 6-2 (on the next page) shows a sample listing obtained by running CHKDSK from drive C. Your listing will show the configuration of your system, which includes the following:

- The name assigned to the disk
- The date of the last disk setup
- A serial number
- Total disk space
- Available disk space
- System memory
- Free memory

CHKDSK also accomplishes a much more important task: It checks the directory table at the beginning of the disk for consistency. Don't be confused by the program name; CHKDSK doesn't really check the entire hard disk. It does examine the directories of the specified disk to see if any clusters are shared by more than one file or if the various clusters for a particular file are not chained together properly.

CHKDSK occasionally displays messages about problems, but don't let that panic you. Most of the time, these problems are caused by abnormal program terminations, such as turning off your computer before quitting the program. The parts of a disk that are questionable are set aside as files with the extension .CHK. You can locate these files and look at them with the Shell.

Chapter 6: At the Command Prompt

```
C:\>CHKDSK

Volume JJ          created 04-11-1991 3:46p
Volume Serial Number is 169E-547A

 64804864 bytes total disk space
   131072 bytes in 5 hidden files
   227328 bytes in 101 directories
 44339200 bytes in 1609 user files
 20107264 bytes available on disk

     2048 bytes in each allocation unit
    31643 total allocation units on disk
     9818 available allocation units on disk

   655360 total bytes memory
   592400 bytes free

C:\>
```

FIGURE 6-2. *A CHKDSK listing.*

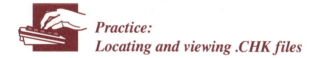
Practice:
Locating and viewing .CHK files

1. If you are at the command prompt, type:

   DOSSHELL

   and press Enter.

2. From the File menu, choose Search.

3. In the Search File dialog box, type:

   *.CHK

   Choose OK or press Enter. If you have no files with the .CHK extension, your screen displays this message:

   No files match file specifier.

   If you do have .CHK files, the screen displays a list of the names.

87

4. Select a file from the list. Then, from the File menu, choose View File Contents.

5. To delete the file, select the name from the list and press Del.

6. Press F3 to return to the command prompt.

In the CHKDSK listing, you might see some space allocated to bad sectors. Don't be alarmed unless this number represents a large percentage of the total disk space. Most disks have a few bad sectors that are "locked out" and not available for use.

VIEWING FILES

At the command prompt, you use the TYPE command to view files. For example, to view the AUTOEXEC.BAT file, type:

    TYPE AUTOEXEC.BAT

at the prompt and press Enter.

COPYING FILES

At the command prompt, you use the COPY command to duplicate files. In general, you need to specify the complete pathname of the source file. However, to copy a file from the current directory, you need not include the directory name. For example, if the current directory is the root directory, type:

    COPY AUTOEXEC.BAT A:

and press Enter to copy AUTOEXEC.BAT to drive A.

In the above example, the destination file has the same name as the source file. To rename the destination file, simply specify the new name after the drive letter, as shown in this example:

    COPY AUTOEXEC.BAT A:TEST.BAT

If the current directory does not contain the source file, you must specify the directory in the pathname. For example, if the current directory is the root directory, type:

    COPY C:\TEST*.* A:

and press Enter to copy all files in a TEST directory in drive C to drive A.

RENAMING FILES

You can rename files using the Shell, but you can do so only one file at a time. Using the DOS RENAME command, you can rename one file at a time or an entire group of files at one time. Again, if the file being renamed is in the current directory, you need not include the directory name in the pathname. The short form of the RENAME command is REN.

To rename a single file, simply type the old name and then the new name after the REN command. For example, to rename the file CHAP5.DOC to CHAP6.DOC, type the following at the prompt and press Enter:

```
REN CHAP5.DOC CHAP6.DOC
```

To rename multiple files, you can use the asterisk wildcard character. For example, to change the extension of all .TXT files in your current directory to .DOC files, type:

```
REN *.TXT *.DOC
```

and press Enter. All the files retain their original filenames, but the names now have the .DOC extension.

Remember that RENAME does not copy or move files; it merely assigns them a new name.

MANAGING DIRECTORIES

At the command prompt, you use the TREE command to take a look at your directory tree. Figure 6-3 (on the following page) shows an example of a directory tree.

NOTE: The TREE command uses graphics characters to display the tree structure. If the structure is not properly shown on your screen, try using the /a parameter (by typing TREE /A) to display text characters only.

DOS includes the following commands for changing directories, making directories, and deleting directories:

- CD   Changes from one directory to another
- MD   Makes a new directory
- RD   Removes (deletes) a directory

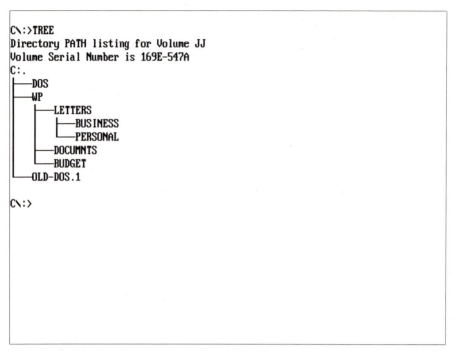

FIGURE 6-3. *A directory tree at the command prompt.*

Changing Directories

The CD command changes the current directory to another directory on the same drive. For example, to change from the root directory to the DOS directory, type:

`CD \DOS`

and press Enter. To verify that you have changed to the DOS directory, use the DIR command.

To change back to the root directory, specify the root directory with a single backslash:

`CD \`

 Typing CD.. *(the CD command followed by two periods) moves you from a subdirectory to its parent directory rather than letting you move directly to the root directory.*

Making a New Directory

The MD command makes a new directory. To make the new directory TEST in the root directory, type:

    MD TEST

at the prompt and press Enter.

Removing a Directory

The RD command deletes a directory. Remember that you can delete a directory only if it contains no files. To delete the TEST directory, type:

    RD TEST

and press Enter.

EDITING AT THE COMMAND PROMPT

The function keys are available for editing at the command prompt, but it can be hard to remember how they all work. The following practice illustrates an easier method.

Practice:
Editing with Doskey

1. At the prompt, type:

   DOSKEY

   and press Enter.

2. Your screen shows the following message:

   DOSKey installed.

3. At the prompt, type:

   DOR/P

   and press Enter.

4. Your screen shows the following message:

   Bad command or file name

5. Press the Up arrow key.

6. Your screen now shows what you originally typed:

   DOR/P

7. Use the Left arrow key to move the cursor to the letter O. Type *I* to correct the command, and then press Enter.

Doskey is a small program that stays in memory until you reboot the computer. To put it in memory each time you boot the computer, include it in your AUTOEXEC.BAT file. (See Chapter 10 and your DOS manual.)

CONTROLLING SCROLLING

Earlier, we used the /p parameter with the DIR command to control the screen display. But the /p parameter is not available for many programs. Instead, you can use a symbol called a pipe along with the DOS filter MORE as the functional equivalent of the /p parameter. To see how this works, type:

   DIR ¦ MORE

at the prompt and press Enter.

The broken vertical bar separating DIR and MORE is the pipe. You type it by holding down the Shift key while you press the backslash key.

MORE is a DOS filter. In the example above, MORE used the directory listing as an input file and directed its output to the screen with a pause. For information on the other DOS filters—SORT and FIND—see your DOS manual.

PRINTING FILES

At the command prompt, you use the PRINT command to print text files, as the following practice illustrates.

Practice:
Printing the AUTOEXEC.BAT file

1. At the prompt, type:

   PRINT AUTOEXEC.BAT

   and press Enter.

2. Your screen shows the following prompt:

   ```
   Name of list device [PRN]:
   ```

   This prompt lets you define the output device, which by default is the printer connected to the parallel printer port; pressing Enter accepts the default device.

3. Press Enter.

FORMATTING A DISK

At the command prompt, you use the FORMAT command to format a hard disk or a floppy disk. The form for this command is the following:

```
FORMAT driveletter:
```

Substitute for *driveletter* the name of the drive containing the disk to be formatted.

If you omit the drive letter, the disk in the current drive is formatted. Remember that formatting a disk erases its entire contents. When using this command, be sure to check the command line before you press Enter—in case you are about to inadvertently format your hard disk. If you do try to format your hard disk, DOS warns you that all data on your hard disk will be lost and gives you a chance to reconsider. Type *N* to abort the formatting.

You can use various options with the FORMAT command to format a disk in special ways. Here are some examples:

FORMAT A: /4	Formats the floppy disk in a high-capacity drive A to 360 KB
FORMAT A: /s	Formats the floppy disk in drive A and copies the operating system to it
FORMAT A: /q	Performs a fast reformat of a previously formatted disk; does not verify the integrity of the disk

MORE ABOUT DOS

The information in this chapter will get you started with the basics of the command prompt. But there's a lot more to learn. For more detailed information, consult the documentation that comes with DOS as well as the references listed in Appendix E of this book.

TIPS ON USING THE COMMAND PROMPT

- Be sure not to start extra copies of the Shell. If you choose Command Prompt from the Shell, you must type *EXIT* at the command prompt to return to the Shell. If you type *DOSSHELL*, you will place another copy of the Shell in the computer's memory, taking memory away from other programs.

- You can get help with any DOS command by typing *HELP* before the command. If you have already typed the command, typing the symbols /? after the command also provides information.

- If you start typing a command at the command prompt but change your mind before pressing Enter, press Esc to cancel the command and start a new line.

- If you made a mistake in typing a command and have already pressed Enter, you do not need to retype the entire line. Press F1 to redisplay the command until you find the error. Press Backspace to delete the error, type the correct letter, and press F1 until the full command is displayed.

- You can change the amount of information provided by the command prompt as well as the look of the prompt by using the DOS PROMPT command.

- The DATE and TIME commands show the date and time according to your computer's clock. If you must reset these values each time you start the computer, you should place these commands in the AUTOEXEC.BAT file.

- If you use a command that displays more than one full screen of information at a time (such as the DIR, TREE, or TYPE command), you can suspend the screen scrolling by pressing Ctrl+S or the Pause key and resume the scrolling by pressing any key. You can terminate the display by pressing Ctrl+C or Ctrl+Break.

- Before you delete files or format disks from the command prompt, you should run the Mirror program. This program helps to accurately restore files when you use the UNDELETE or the UNFORMAT command.

- You can rename, copy, move, or delete multiple files from the command prompt by using wildcard characters in the filenames.
- The DOS PRINT command causes files to be printed using a print queue—that is, you can list numerous files, and they will be printed in the order listed. You can even continue working on your computer while the files are being printed.
- You can save keystrokes and execute multiple commands by running batch files at the command prompt. (See Chapter 9.)

Chapter 7

Protecting Your Data

An old computer cliché claims that there are two kinds of computer users—those whose hard disk has crashed and those whose hard disk is going to crash. Computers are so reliable today that we tend to think our data is safe once it is on a disk. Moreover, backing up data takes time that we'd rather spend doing productive work. The truth is, however, that computers do lose data, and the results can be catastrophic. Companies have gone bankrupt from the loss of computer data. But you don't have to lose data when a disk crashes. This chapter tells you how to protect your data.

PREVENTING DATA LOSS

To simplify the discussion, let's assume that disk crashes are hardware related, software related, or user related.

Hardware-Related Causes

In most cases, the failure of a computer component does not cause any loss of data. After the machine is fixed, the data is still on the hard disk. But if the hard disk itself fails or if the failure of another computer component causes data corruption, you can be in trouble.

If the computer acts a little strange, immediately back up all data. (See "Backing Up Data," later in this chapter.) If you take the computer in for repair, first back up all data. In either case, don't back up to the disks or tape containing the last backup. Instead, use fresh disks or tapes.

You can also lose data as a result of system overheating, noise on the power line, power surges, or static electricity. Here are some ways to protect against data loss caused by hardware:

- Always turn on the system unit last and turn it off first so that noise or surges from the printer or the console will not affect the hard-disk data in the system unit.

- Use a noise and surge protector, and plug all computer components into it. Be sure that the incoming power has a true ground (three-wire or separate grounding). A surge suppressor is a special device that protects the system from noise and other problems on the power line. It's very cheap insurance for what it does, but check to be sure that it protects against both noise and surges, which are two different things.

- Unplug the system (all components) during an electrical storm. If power fluctuates, turn off your computer equipment.

- Use an antistatic mat under the computer desk. Static electricity can build up on your body if the humidity is low or if you are wearing clothing made of synthetic materials. When you touch the keyboard, static electricity is discharged through the computer.

- If you open the computer to work on it, unplug all power cables and ground your body. The easiest way to do this is to run a clip wire from your watchband to a ground.
- Be sure that air circulates around the computer. Periodically clean the external area around computer fans and vent holes with a vacuum cleaner.
- Treat all disks with care. Don't subject hard disks to any mechanical shock, and keep floppy disks away from magnetic fields such as telephones, speakers, and desk lamps.
- Back up your data often.
- When moving a computer, turn it off, place empty floppy disks in each drive, and close the latches. Doing so protects the read/write heads of the drive.

Software-Related Causes

Occasionally a program instruction becomes garbled or altered, but the computer continues to try to follow the garbled instruction. Most of the time, the computer then simply locks up or does something unusual. In rare cases, however, a garbled instruction can cause data loss.

Software-related problems can be intentional or unintentional. For example, a program you have been using for months suddenly misbehaves. You reinstall it, and it works fine. Or perhaps you install a program and a week later discover that the program is corrupting your disk. In both cases, the damage is unintentional but nevertheless real.

Intentional damage is a growing menace and is usually caused by a virus. A virus is computer code (a set of instructions) designed to reproduce, survive, and be nonproductive. The code is passed between computers as a part of valid programs and attempts to remain active until it has accomplished its task, which can be anything from displaying a humorous message to causing major data loss.

Here are some ways to protect against data loss caused by software:

- Back up your data frequently.
- When you obtain free software or obtain software from a bulletin board, always check the software for viruses before using it. Most bulletin boards have virus-checking programs you can download.

- Never install from the original floppy disks of copy-protected programs. If an instruction in such a program becomes garbled, or if the hard disk fails, you generally cannot reinstall the program to the disk. Copy the originals, and install from the copy.

- When installing programs from floppy disks, always write-protect the disks before using them. If the installation process needs to write to the disks, copy the write-protected masters and install the program from the copies.

User-Related Causes

A user, quite unintentionally, can also cause data loss. Here are some ways this can happen and suggestions about how to recover data:

- You intend to delete only a file or two, but instead you accidentally delete additional files or the entire floppy disk or hard disk. Delete files with caution. When you see the Confirmation dialog box in the Shell or the command prompt message, take time to read the filenames listed for deletion. If an accidental deletion occurs, don't write anything to the disk until your files are recovered. The data is still on the disk; it is simply missing from the directory. You can try to recover the lost files by using the Shell's Undelete program from the Disk Utilities program group or the DOS UNDELETE command at the command prompt (discussed later in this chapter). If this fails, recover the data from a backup disk.

- You unintentionally turn off the computer, reboot, or terminate a program when working with a data file. The data might be in a temporary file on the disk. If necessary, call the software manufacturer to find out how to locate and use the temporary file. Some programs back up each time you save a file. You might find a file that is incomplete or old, but it's better than having nothing.

BACKING UP DATA

The reason backups are so important is, of course, that you can recover data from them. The strategy you use for backing up your data is also important.

Types of Backup

You can back up to disks or tape. Backups can be full, partial, incremental, differential, or dated:

Full	Backs up all files
Partial	Backs up a set of files or a directory
Incremental	Backs up files changed since the last backup of any type
Differential	Backs up files changed since the last full backup
Dated	Backs up files changed since a specified date

Which type of backup you use depends on your specific needs and on how you use your computer. Here are some backup tips:

- Always keep a full backup of your hard disk, including program files. Program files don't change often, but you still need the backup.
- Use caution in mixing backup types. Don't, for example, mix incremental and differential backups.
- Set up a schedule for backing up the disk, and stick to it.
- Use multiple levels of backups. For example, if you did a full backup last Friday and plan to do another full backup this Friday, don't use the same disks. Use multiple disk sets, and always back up to the oldest.
- Keep backup disks or tapes at a location away from the computer.
- If your hard disk starts to go down or an erratic problem begins to occur, make a backup immediately. Use fresh floppy disks or tapes. Keep the previous backup in case the data is already partially or totally corrupted.
- Always label your backup disks and tapes. Include the date and the type of backup.

How Often to Back Up

How often you need to back up your hard disk depends on how you use the system. If you use programs that don't change often, you might need a full backup only a few times a year. In the meantime, a differential or dated backup might be sufficient. If you keep projects in progress in specific directories, back up these directories to a floppy disk once a day when you are working on them. The basic rule is to ask yourself this question: If the computer goes down tonight, how much data will I lose? If it would take considerable time to reenter the data or if the data could not be recovered at all, back it up.

Backup Methods

The simplest way to back up files is to copy them to a floppy disk. (This method is practical only for backups that fit on a single floppy disk.) You can use the COPY command at the command prompt, or you can use the Shell.

For more general backups, use Backup Fixed Disk from the Shell's Disk Utilities program group. We will describe and use this program later in this chapter. It does, however, have some disadvantages: It doesn't compress any files, which means that you will need a lot of floppies; it is slow; and its options are limited.

If you have a large hard disk and many files to back up, you might want to purchase a file compression and archival program. These programs take out all the "extra space" in files and can substantially reduce the total size of a file: Text files are often reduced by 30 percent or more, and many graphics files are reduced by more than 90 percent.

Alternatively, if you have a large hard disk and get tired of changing floppies, you can purchase a tape backup system. These systems are available from various manufacturers, with various storage capacities. The tape drive comes with its own software. A tape system isn't as reliable as a good floppy-disk backup system, but it is dramatically faster and (if the tape has enough storage) can be run without user intervention. If you use tape, however, be sure that you verify after making the backup.

You can also use Backup Fixed Disk to back up floppy disks. This method is useful if you want to back up only files that have been changed since a certain date or since the last backup. To back up an entire floppy disk, however, you'll usually find it easier to use the DOS command DISKCOPY, COPY, or XCOPY.

GETTING STARTED WITH MS-DOS 5 AND THE *NEW* MS-DOS SHELL

MAKING BACKUPS

Now let's use the Shell to make a full backup.

Preparing for Backup

First, you must figure out how many floppy disks you will need.

Practice:
Determining the number of floppies for a full backup

1. Select drive C from the drive list.
2. From the View menu, choose All Files. Now look at the lower left portion of the screen, under the heading Disk, and record both the value for Size (the number of bytes on the disk) and the value for Avail (the number of free bytes left on the disk):

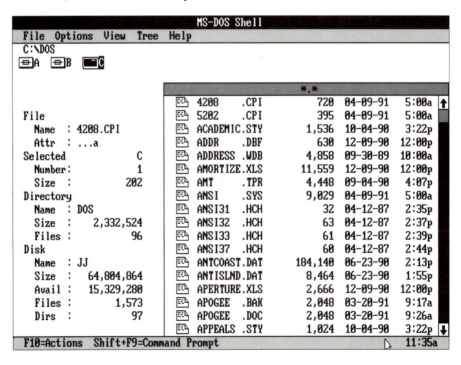

3. Subtract Avail from Size to get the number of bytes you have used.

104

4. Use this table to find out approximately how many floppies you will need for each 10 megabytes of hard-disk space you have used:

Disk Type	Number of Floppy Disks Required
3½-inch (720 KB)	15
3½-inch (1.44 MB)	8
5¼-inch (360 KB)	29
5¼-inch (1.2 MB)	9

Don't format the floppy disks, but do put labels on them. Number them sequentially, and record the date and time of the backup on the labels.

5. From the View menu, choose Program/File Lists.

Backing Up

The following practice shows you step by step how to back up your hard-disk drive. If at any time you want to halt the backup, press Ctrl+C.

Practice:
Backing up drive C

1. In the Program list area, choose Disk Utilities from the Main program group if Disk Utilities is not already active.

2. From the Disk Utilities program group, choose Backup Fixed Disk.

3. The Backup Fixed Disk dialog box appears. The default parameters it contains tell DOS to back up all files on drive C to the floppy disks in drive A.

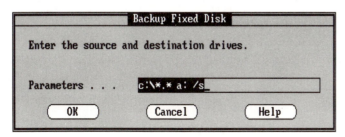

GETTING STARTED WITH MS-DOS 5 AND THE *NEW* MS-DOS SHELL

4. Press Enter or choose OK.

5. Your screen shows the following message:

   Insert backup diskette 01 in drive A:

6. Place disk 01 in drive A, and press any key. If the disk is not formatted, DOS formats it before copying files to it. As DOS copies the files, the filenames appear on your screen. You are prompted when it is time to insert the next disk.

7. When the backup is complete, press any key to return to the Shell.

Notice that the default parameter in the Backup Fixed Disk dialog box is /s. Here is a list of the available parameters:

/s	Backs up subdirectories and files
/m	Backs up files changed since the last backup
/a	Adds backup files to existing files on the floppy disks
/d:<*date*>	Backs up files modified since *date*
/t:<*time*>	Backs up files modified since *time*
/l:<*xxxx*>	Creates a log file in path *xxxx*
/f:<*size*>	Formats the destination disk to *size*

NOTE: System files are not backed up when you run the Backup Fixed Disk program. Unless you use the /a parameter, old backup files on a floppy disk are erased. Avoid mixing the Backup and Restore programs from different versions of DOS.

You should always have a backup of your DOS system files on a floppy disk, in case something happens to the system files on your hard disk. Use the SYS command from the command prompt to back up these files.

Practice:
Backing up a single directory

1. In the Program list area, choose Disk Utilities from the Main program group if Disk Utilities is not already active.

Chapter 7: Protecting Your Data

2. From the Disk Utilities program group, choose Backup Fixed Disk.

3. In the Backup Fixed Disk dialog box, type:

   `C:\`*directoryname* `A:`

   substituting for *directoryname* the name of the directory to be backed up. Choose OK or press Enter.

4. Your screen displays this message:

   `Insert backup diskette 01 in drive A:`

5. Insert the floppy disk, and press any key.

6. When the backup is complete, press any key to return to the Shell.

RESTORING A DISK

The easiest way to restore a single file to your disk from a backup floppy is simply to copy it. If your files were backed up using Backup Fixed Disk, you should use Restore Fixed Disk from the Shell's Disk Utilities program group. In the Restore Fixed Disk dialog box, enter the source and destination drives, and then press Enter or choose OK:

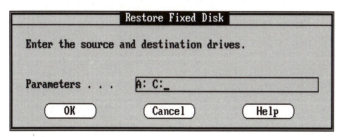

In the example above, all files on the floppy disk in drive A are being restored to drive C.

To recover all files from a set of disks, specify only the drives as parameters (no wildcards):

   `A: C:`

DOS places the files in the correct directory.

107

You can use these parameters in the Restore Fixed Disk dialog box:

/p	Prompts the user for permission to restore if the file is marked read-only on the target disk or if the target disk copy has a later date
/n	Restores only the files that are not on the target disk
/m	Restores files not on the target disk or files changed since the last backup
/b:<date>	Restores files created or modified on or before *date*
/a:<date>	Restores files created or modified on or after *date*
/e:<time>	Restores files created or modified at or before *time*
/l:<time>	Restores files created or modified at or after *time*
/s	Restores subdirectories

NOTE: You can use Restore Fixed Disk to restore files from floppy disks made with any previous version of DOS, but you cannot use it to restore system files.

Assuming that your entire hard disk is backed up, here are the basic steps to restore it:

1. Reinstall DOS on the hard disk, and verify that it is working correctly.
2. Use Restore Fixed Disk from the Disk Utilities program group to restore the entire disk.

RECOVERING FILES

If you accidentally delete files, you might be able to recover them using Undelete from the Disk Utilities program group or the UNDELETE command from the command prompt. When you delete files, the files are not physically removed from the disk. The filenames are simply marked to indicate that the disk space is available for reuse. If nothing has been written to the disk space where the files were located, and if the directory in which the files resided has not been deleted, you might be able to recover the deleted files.

When you accidentally delete a file, stop whatever you are doing and try to recover the file immediately, before anything can be written to its disk space. You should have backup copies of all important files in case you cannot successfully undelete a file.

Practice:
Listing deleted files with Undelete

1. In the Program list area, choose Disk Utilities from the Main program group if Disk Utilities is not already active.

2. From the Disk Utilities program group, choose Undelete.

3. The Undelete dialog box displays the parameter /list. Press Enter or choose OK to see a list of deleted files.

If you want to recover all the listed files, use the parameter /all instead of /list in the Undelete dialog box. The program then successively displays the name of each deleted file and asks if you want to undelete the file. If you want to recover all the deleted files in the current directory only, do not use any parameters in the Undelete dialog box.

You can also undelete a single specific file or a group of files by using the UNDELETE command from the command prompt. After typing the command, specify the path and filename of the file to be undeleted, and then press Enter. For a group of files, use wildcard characters in the filename.

If you accidentally reformat your hard disk, you might be able to recover it using the DOS UNFORMAT command. See your DOS manual for details.

NOTE: DOS keeps track of deleted files in two ways: with the File Allocation Table and with the Mirror program. The Mirror program produces a file that lists all deleted files and makes recovering them easier and more reliable than if DOS had to depend only on the File Allocation Table. The Mirror program automatically starts if you use the Shell, but it must be started with a command if you are working only from the DOS command prompt. Your DOS manual contains more information on the Mirror program.

TIPS ON PROTECTING DATA

- If you enter large amounts of data every day—into a database management program, for example—back up your data at the end of each day, no matter how much you might be tempted to take a chance and skip this chore. The cost of reentering the data is enormous compared with the time required to back it up.

- Be sure to include the date on the label of every backup disk. You might even want to include the time of the backup.

- If you are entering data that is impossible to recapture, consider making two backups and keeping each in a separate place.

- Weather can cause power fluctuations that in turn can cause your computer system to malfunction. In an office environment, assign someone to sound the alert when the weather turns threatening—especially to warn those in windowless offices.

- If you process sensitive data—for example, personnel information—protect those files with a password (if the application permits it), and keep your system in a locked location.

Chapter 8

Introduction to the Editor

The MS-DOS Editor is a simple word processor that you can use to read, edit, create, and print text files and batch files. An editor differs from a word processor in two primary ways: First, an editor lacks formatting capability; second, an editor does not wordwrap. This means that you can't select fonts or set margins, for example, and that you must press Enter to end a line (just as you use the carriage return on a typewriter). You can, however, cut and paste and search and replace with an editor as you can with a word processor.

STARTING THE EDITOR

You can start the Editor with any of these four methods:

- From the Main program group in the Program list area, choose the Editor.
- From the File list, choose EDIT.COM.
- From the File menu, choose Run, and then type *EDIT.COM* in the Run dialog box.
- At the DOS command prompt, type *EDIT.COM*.

If you start the Editor from the Main program group, the File to Edit dialog box appears on your screen. You have the following options:

- To create a new file or to edit an existing file, type the filename and then press Enter or choose OK.
- To start the Editor without a file, press Enter or choose OK. When the Editor starts, press Esc to clear the screen.

You can have a file already loaded when you start the Editor from the File list, from the Run dialog box, or from the command prompt. With the File list, choose the text file you want to edit. If it has the .TXT file extension, it will start in the Editor. In the Run dialog box or after the command prompt, type *EDIT.COM*, add a space, and then type the filename.

Typing the full pathname of a file ensures that the file will be found. If you type only the filename of a file that is not located in the current directory, the Editor will open a blank document.

LOOKING AT THE EDITOR SCREEN

Figure 8-1 (on the following page) shows the Editor screen. You choose from menus on this screen, as you do in the Shell window, although the two groups of menus are somewhat different. To get Help, press F1. To exit the Editor, choose Exit from the File menu.

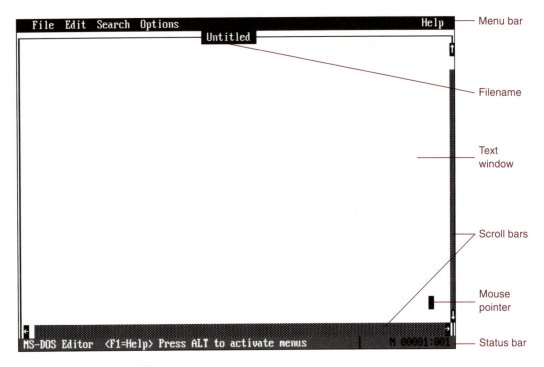

FIGURE 8-1. *The Editor screen.*

MANAGING FILES WITH THE EDITOR

You use the File menu to create a file, open a file, edit a file, save a file, or print a file.

Practice:
Opening a file when you start the Editor

1. Select the DOS directory in the Directory Tree.
2. In the Program list area, choose the Main program group if it is not already active.
3. From the Main program group, choose the Editor.

Chapter 8: Introduction to the Editor

4. In the File to Edit dialog box, type:

   README.TXT

   and press Enter or choose OK. (README.TXT is an information file that is part of the DOS 5 Shell.)

Notice that a blinking underline cursor marks the insertion point. If you have a mouse, you also see the rectangular mouse cursor because the Editor runs in text mode only. To move the insertion point, select a new insertion point with the mouse or use the arrow keys.

Practice:
Editing README.TXT with the mouse

1. Start the Editor, and open the README.TXT file if you have not already done so.

2. To scroll down one line at a time, click the Down arrow in the scroll bar.

3. To select the first word, click on the first character. Then hold down the mouse button, and drag the mouse cursor past the last character. Release the mouse button.

4. To delete this word, press Del.

5. Now type the deleted word to reinsert it.

6. To select five consecutive lines of text, click on any character in the first line, hold down the Shift key, and then click on any character in the last line.

7. From the Edit menu, choose Cut to move this selection. Move the cursor to the new location, and, from the Edit menu, choose Paste.

8. From the File menu, choose Exit. Now choose No to avoid saving your changes to the original README.TXT file.

Practice:
Editing README.TXT with the keyboard

1. Start the Editor, and open the README.TXT file.

2. To move the insertion point, use the arrow keys to move one line or one character at a time.

3. To move up or down one screenful at a time, press PgUp or PgDn.

4. To select the first word, use the arrow keys to move the insertion point to the first character. Hold down Shift, and move the insertion point to the last character.

5. To delete this word, press Del.

6. Now type the deleted word to reinsert it.

7. To select five consecutive lines of text, use the arrow keys to move the insertion point to the first line. Hold down Shift, and press the Down arrow key to select the other lines, one line at a time.

8. From the Edit menu, choose Cut to move this selection. Use the arrow keys to move the insertion point to the new location, and, from the Edit menu, choose Paste.

9. From the File menu, choose Exit. Now choose No to avoid saving your changes to the original README.TXT file.

In the Editor, you can also use the following keys and key combinations:

Backspace	Deletes the character to the left of the cursor
Ctrl+T	Deletes the word at the cursor
Ins	Toggles insert mode
Ctrl+Left arrow	Moves the cursor one word to the left
Ctrl+Right arrow	Moves the cursor one word to the right
Home	Moves the cursor to the beginning of the line
End	Moves the cursor to the end of the line
Ctrl+Home	Moves the cursor to the beginning of the file
Ctrl+End	Moves the cursor to the end of the file

Chapter 8: Introduction to the Editor

 When you start the Editor, it is in insert mode—that is, the characters you type are inserted at the insertion point, and existing text moves to the right. To change to overwrite mode, press Ins. Now the characters you type replace existing characters at the insertion point. To change back to insert mode, press Ins again.

 Practice:
Creating, saving, and printing a file

1. In the Program list area, choose the Main program group if it is not already active.

2. From the Main program group, choose the Editor.

3. In the File to Edit dialog box, type:

   NEW.TXT

   and press Enter or choose OK.

4. You can now enter text. Remembering to press Enter to end each line, type the following:

   ```
   Jonathan Swift summed up editorial work as follows:
   Blot out, correct, insert, refine,
   Enlarge, diminish, interline;
   Be mindful, when invention fails,
   To scratch your head, and bite your nails.
   ```

5. From the File menu, choose Save.

6. Now from the File menu, choose Print.

7. In the Print dialog box, Complete Document is selected by default. Choose OK or press Enter.

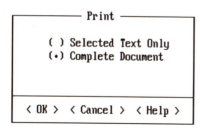

117

NOTE: Files are printed only to the primary parallel printer port (LPT1). If your printer is not connected to this port, you cannot print from the Editor unless you redirect the printer through LPT1; see your DOS manual for information.

Practice:
Copying a block of text

1. Select the first line of the file NEW.TXT.
2. From the Edit menu, choose Copy.
3. Move the insertion point to the line below the last line of text.
4. From the Edit menu, choose Paste.

SEARCHING AND REPLACING

Finding and changing a word or phrase throughout a small file such as NEW.TXT is simple. But in a large file, trying to manually find all occurrences of a string of text and change them to something else can be time consuming—not to mention the risk of overlooking some occurrences. You can, however, use the Editor to search and replace quickly and accurately.

Practice:
Searching for "Running"

1. Open the README.TXT file.
2. From the Search menu, choose Find.
3. In the Find dialog box (shown on the next page), type *Running* in the Find What: field, and then press Enter or choose OK.

    If you also select the Match Upper/Lowercase check box, you find only text that exactly matches what you typed. If you select Whole Word, you find only matches that are whole words. If neither option is selected, you find all occurrences of the text you typed, whether they contain uppercase or lowercase letters or whether they are whole words or part of other words.

Chapter 8: Introduction to the Editor

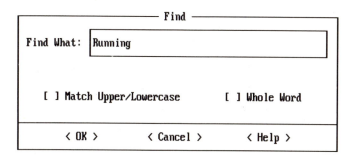

 NOTE: *When you search with the Find command, only one occurrence of the text initially appears on the screen. To find the next occurrence, choose Repeat Last Find from the Search menu or press F3.*

Practice:
Finding "Running" and changing it to "Starting"

1. Open the README.TXT file if it is not already open.
2. From the Search menu, choose Change.
3. In the Change dialog box, type *Running* in the Find What: field. In the Change To: field, type *Starting*.

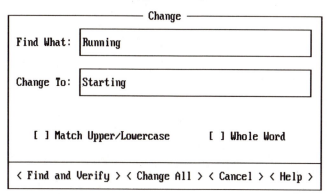

If you then choose the Change All command button, all occurrences of "Running" are changed to "Starting" without your intervention. For now, choose the Find and Verify command button so that the Editor will give you an opportunity to confirm that you really want to change each occurrence.

119

4. A new Change dialog box appears, in which you can choose Change or Skip as each occurrence of "Running" is highlighted. (Choose Skip for now.) Notice that this dialog box moves around on your screen to allow you to see the text that is about to be changed.

5. When all occurrences of "Running" have been found, the dialog box informs you that all changes have been completed. Choose OK or press Enter.

If you select a word or other block of text before choosing the Find command or the Change command, the text appears in the dialog box.

CUSTOMIZING THE EDITOR

Using the Options menu, you can change the colors of the text window, set tab stops, and turn the scroll bars on or off.

1. From the Options menu, choose Display.

2. The Display dialog box appears. (See Figure 8-2 on the next page.) As you select various foreground and background colors, the box on the left shows how your colors appear on the screen. By default, the Scroll Bars option is turned on. If you turn this option off, scroll bars will not appear on your screen. Also by default, tab stops are set at eight-character intervals. To change this setting, simply type a new number in the Tab Stops: field.

3. When you complete your selections, press Enter or choose OK.

4. From the File menu, choose Exit to quit the Editor. If the Editor asks whether you want to save the file, choose No.

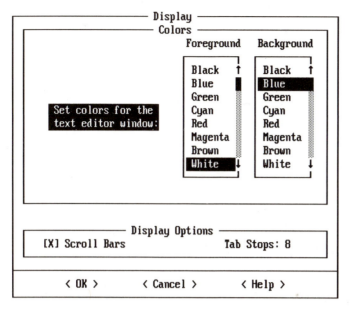

FIGURE 8-2. *The Display dialog box.*

TIPS ON USING THE EDITOR

- Using the Editor to change or create a simple .TXT file or a .BAT file can be faster than loading your word processor and the file.

- If you don't have a word processing program, using the Editor is a good way to learn how simple word processors work.

- You can use the Editor to create and print any document for which formatting is not important.

Chapter 9

The Basics of Batch Files

A batch file is a text file that contains a sequence of DOS commands. The primary use of a batch file is to simplify tasks that you carry out frequently. All batch files have the filename extension .BAT.

Chapter 9: The Basics of Batch Files

In previous chapters, we've used one of the most common batch files—AUTOEXEC.BAT—to illustrate various concepts and to show you how certain features of the Shell work. This file executes whenever you start or reboot your system, and it must be in the root directory of the disk from which you boot DOS.

To see how easy it is to create a batch file and to get an idea of how batch files can make using your computer easier and faster, let's create a file that you can use to start the Shell from the command prompt with one keystroke.

Practice:
Creating D.BAT

1. From the Main program group in the Program list area, choose the Editor.

2. In the File to Edit dialog box, type:

   D.BAT

   and press Enter or choose OK.

3. Now, in the Editor screen, type:

   DOSSHELL

4. From the File menu, choose Save.

5. From the File menu, choose Exit to exit the Editor.

To see how D.BAT works, press F3 to exit the Shell. Then, at the command prompt, type:

   D

and press Enter. The Shell starts.

WHY USE BATCH FILES?

- Batch files save time. Putting many commands in a single file that you can execute with one keystroke or even several keystrokes is much faster than typing all the commands individually.

- Batch files improve accuracy. After you create a batch file and ensure that it is error free, you eliminate the possibility of making a typo when you enter a series of commands. In addition, whatever task the batch file performs is always done in the same manner each time—until you change the batch file.

- Batch files simplify tasks. You need not remember all the necessary command sequences or how they work every time you want to repeat a task.

CAUTION: A batch file, like any other type of computer programming, can produce unexpected results if the program contains any errors. Be sure that your files are backed up before you use a batch file for the first time.

CREATING BATCH FILES

You can create or modify batch files with any word processor that can create text-only files and with the DOS Editor. In this chapter, we will use the Editor, but you can use whichever method you prefer.

Backing up your files is an important task that must be performed frequently. For example, as this book was written, word processing files were created for each chapter. The following practice shows you the batch file that was used to back up all chapters at the end of each working day and to delete the temporary backup files from the hard disk.

Practice:
Creating BACKUP.BAT

1. From the Main program group in the Program list area, choose the Editor.

2. In the File to Edit dialog box, type:

   BACKUP.BAT

   and press Enter or choose OK.

3. Now, in the Editor screen, type:

   COPY C:\WP\CHAP*.DOC A:
   DEL C:\WP\CHAP*.BAK

4. From the File menu, choose Save.

This version of BACKUP.BAT assumes that you have a WP directory and files whose names begin with CHAP and end with .DOC or .BAK extensions. To make the batch file work on your computer, change the directory name and the filenames to match the path and filenames you use.

RUNNING BATCH FILES

You can run batch files from the command prompt, from the File menu, from the File list, or from the Program list. In the first practice in this chapter, you ran D.BAT from the command prompt. To run batch files from the Program list, you must put them in a program group. (See Chapter 5 if you need help with this.)

DOS maintains a temporary file on the current directory to keep track of a running batch file. When the batch file terminates, the temporary file is erased.

To terminate a batch file before it completes, press Ctrl+Break or Ctrl+C. If you are running the batch file from the command prompt, the following prompt appears:

```
Terminate batch job (Y/N)?
```

Press Y to ignore the rest of the batch file and return to DOS.

If you are running the batch file from the Shell, pressing Ctrl+Break or Ctrl+C terminates the batch file and returns you to the Shell.

SPECIAL BATCH COMMANDS

In addition to the standard DOS commands, your batch file can include a set of special commands.

The ECHO Command

Normally, as you execute a batch file, you see each command on the screen. You can, however, turn off this display with the ECHO OFF command. Let's add ECHO OFF to BACKUP.BAT. Remember that you can modify any batch file with the Editor.

Practice:
Modifying BACKUP.BAT

1. From the Main program group in the Program list area, choose the Editor.

2. In the File to Edit dialog box, type:

   BACKUP.BAT

   and press Enter or choose OK.

3. Add the following line above the existing first line:

   ECHO OFF

4. From the File menu, choose Save.

Now exit the Editor, and run BACKUP.BAT to see how it works. Notice that you see the filenames as they are copied but that the commands (except the ECHO OFF command) do not appear on the screen.

You can use the ECHO command to display a message on the screen. For example, add the following text as the second line of BACKUP.BAT:

ECHO Backup Book Files

You can also keep the ECHO OFF command from being displayed on the screen by adding an at sign (@) before the command:

@ECHO OFF

Now the BACKUP.BAT file reads as follows:

```
@ECHO OFF
ECHO Backup Book Files
COPY C:\WP\CHAP*.DOC A:
DEL C:\WP\CHAP*.BAK
```

After you save this modified batch file, it will run without displaying any of the commands, but it will display for the user a message that describes the purpose of the file.

The REM Command

You use the REM (REMARK) command to place comments in a batch file. Comments do not affect how the file works; they simply contain information about the file that might be of future use to you or to someone who wants to understand the structure of the file. The REM command is particularly helpful in long files. Although we don't really need it in such a short file, let's place a REM command in BACKUP.BAT as a new second line. Now your file looks like this:

```
@ECHO OFF
REM Daily backup for book files
ECHO Backup Book Files
COPY C:\WP\CHAP*.DOC A:
DEL C:\WP\CHAP*.BAK
```

REM statements are displayed if ECHO is on and hidden if ECHO is off.

Use the REMARK command frequently to remind yourself of the purpose of the batch file and its steps. You can also use this command to record your name and the dates of any changes in the file for other users.

The PAUSE Command

When you want to give the user an opportunity to make a decision or perform a task, you can insert the PAUSE command in a batch file. Then, at that point in the execution of the batch file, PAUSE will display the following message on the screen:

```
Press any key to continue...
```

You can, however, display other messages by using the ECHO command before the PAUSE command in the batch file, as shown in this example:

```
ECHO Place a diskette in drive A
PAUSE
```

Add the two lines above to BACKUP.BAT and save the file:

```
@ECHO OFF
REM Daily backup for book files
ECHO Backup Book Files
ECHO Place a diskette in drive A
PAUSE
COPY C:\WP\CHAP*.DOC A:
DEL C:\WP\CHAP*.BAK
```

Now when you run BACKUP.BAT, the screen displays this message before copying the files:

```
Backup Book Files
Place a diskette in drive A
Press any key to continue...
```

The CLS Command

The CLS command clears the screen. It is often used as the last command in the AUTOEXEC.BAT file. CLS does not clear memory or delete files; it simply clears the screen and returns the user to the DOS prompt. Add CLS now as the last line in BACKUP.BAT, save the file, and then run it again.

The GOTO Command

The GOTO command tells DOS to go to a specific line in the batch file, rather than to the next command in the sequence, and resume execution. The following batch file makes several copies of a floppy disk and uses the GOTO command to let the user know when one copy is complete and a new floppy disk should be inserted:

```
@ECHO OFF
REM Make multiple copies of a floppy disk
:repeat
ECHO Insert the source disk in drive A
PAUSE Insert the destination disk in drive B
COPY A: B:
ECHO Press Ctrl+Break to quit
PAUSE
GOTO repeat
```

This chapter explains only the basics of batch files, helping you understand the concept and some possible uses of these files. For more information on making and using batch files, see your DOS manual and other books on DOS listed in Appendix E of this book.

TIPS ON USING BATCH FILES

- You can create a batch file with any word processor that saves files as text files, but you must use the .BAT—not the .DOC—extension with the filename.

- When naming batch files, be sure to use terms that accurately and clearly describe the function of the batch file.

- When you run a batch file from the DOS command prompt or from the Run dialog box (from the File menu), you do not need to include the .BAT extension when you type the filename. This allows you to use filenames that are descriptive and as simple as DOS command names.

- A batch file is suspended when an executable file is run, but the batch file is resumed when that program is completed. For example, if a batch file calls your word processor, the batch file is resumed when you quit the word processor.

- You can have one batch file run a second batch file by including the name of the second file as the last item in the first batch file.

Chapter 10

Customizing Your System

You can customize your system from the Shell and from the command prompt. From the Shell, you can change colors and display mode, control confirmation messages, enable or disable the Task Swapper, and determine program groups. From the command prompt, you can set the system date and time, choose a prompt, and alter disk and memory management.

Chapter 10: Customizing Your System

CUSTOMIZING FROM THE SHELL

From the Shell, you can control the display, establish the level of confirmation, toggle the Task Swapper, and specify how lists of your files and programs appear on the screen.

Controlling the Display

You use the Options menu to set colors and mode.

Practice:
Changing screen colors

1. From the Options menu, choose Colors.
2. In the Color Scheme dialog box, scroll the list to see the available color schemes.
3. To see how a color scheme looks without choosing it, select the scheme and then choose Preview.
4. To choose a scheme, select it, and then choose OK or press Enter.

As you know, you can use the Shell in either text mode or graphics mode. Most of the illustrations in Chapter 1 show the screen in text mode; illustrations in the rest of the chapters show the screen in graphics mode.

Practice:
Changing mode

1. From the Options menu, choose Display.
2. In the Screen Display Mode dialog box, select from the mode list.
3. To see how a mode displays without choosing it, choose Preview.
4. To choose a mode, select it, and then choose OK or press Enter.

NOTE: The available screen modes depend on the type of video adapter you have. To change the list in the Screen Display Mode dialog box, you must reinstall DOS for a different adapter.

135

Color and mode options are stored in the DOSSHELL.INI file, which you can view and edit with the Editor. This file also defines program groups.

 If you edit the DOSSHELL.INI file, first make a backup. Then, if something goes wrong, you can restore the original file by copying the backup to DOSSHELL.INI.

Controlling the Level of Confirmation

When you install the Shell, all confirmation options are turned on by default. For example, when you delete a file or a directory, a dialog box appears, asking whether you really want to delete the item. Confirmation dialog boxes give you the opportunity to change your mind—just in case you selected an option in error or have second thoughts about the action you are about to take.

If you feel comfortable working without these second chances, you can turn off the Confirmation dialog boxes. And, if you change your mind, you can always turn them back on.

Practice:
Turning off Confirmation dialog boxes

1. From the Options menu, choose Confirmation. The Confirmation dialog box appears:

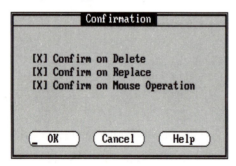

2. In the dialog box, turn off the check boxes by deleting the Xs (clicking on the Xs or pressing Spacebar).

3. Choose OK or press Enter.

The Shell will no longer display the Delete File Confirmation dialog box, the Replace File Confirmation dialog box, or the Confirm Mouse Operation dialog box. If you decide that you do want confirmation, restore it by checking these boxes (restoring the Xs) in the Confirmation dialog box.

Controlling the Task Swapper

To use the multitasking feature of the Shell, you must enable the Task Swapper. Doing so opens the Active Task List (discussed in Chapter 5).

Controlling the View

With the Shell, you have five ways of looking at your files and programs. Choose the view you want from the View menu.

If you choose Single File List, your screen display is similar to Figure 10-1. In Single File List view, the Program list area and the Active Task List are not displayed. (In Figure 10-1, the Task Swapper is enabled, as it is in the subsequent screen illustrations in this section.)

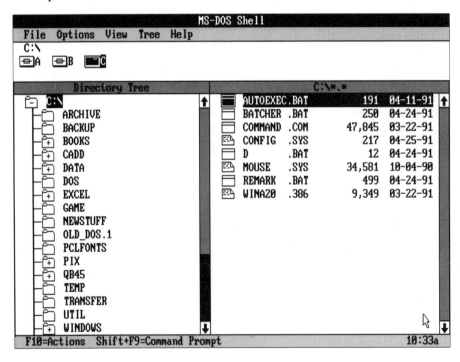

FIGURE 10-1. *Single File List view.*

If you choose Dual File Lists, your screen display is similar to Figure 10-2. The Dual File Lists view is useful when you copy or move files. In this view, the Program list area and the Active Task List are not displayed.

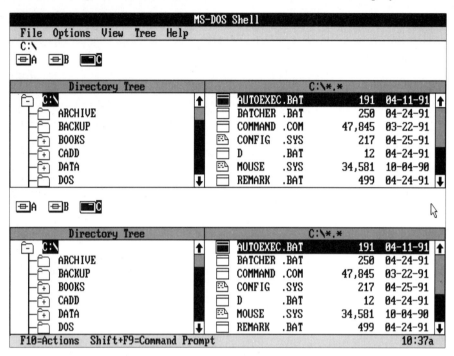

FIGURE 10-2. *Dual File Lists view.*

Chapter 10: Customizing Your System

If you choose All Files, your screen display is similar to Figure 10-3. The All Files view fills the entire screen and shows all files and directories on a disk. The Program list area and the Active Task List are not displayed.

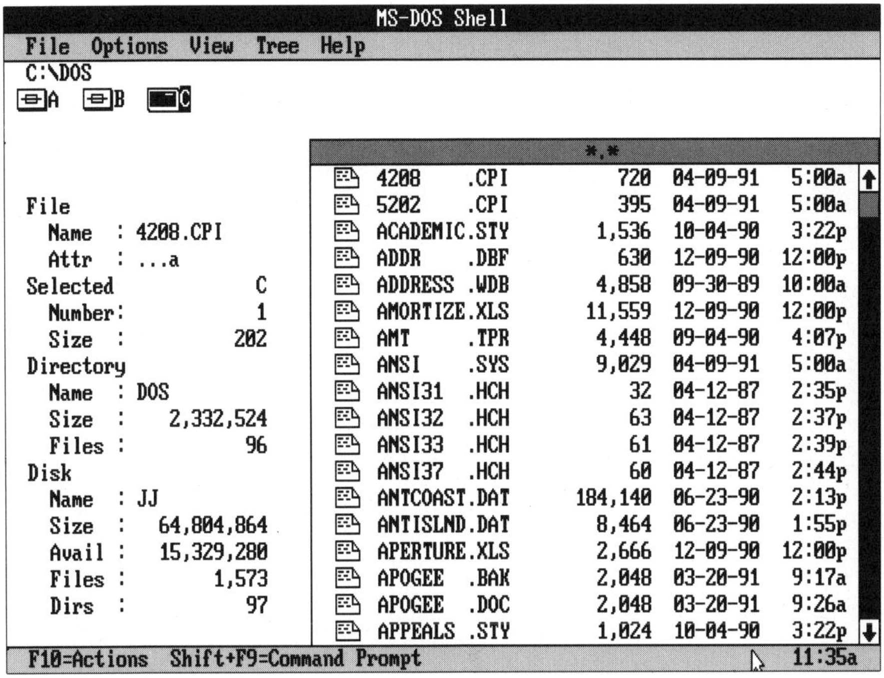

```
                              MS-DOS Shell
 File  Options  View  Tree  Help
 C:\DOS
 [=]A  [=]B  [=]C
                                                   *.*
                             4208      .CPI        720    04-09-91   5:00a
 File                        5202      .CPI        395    04-09-91   5:00a
   Name : 4208.CPI           ACADEMIC  .STY      1,536    10-04-90   3:22p
   Attr :  ...a              ADDR      .DBF        630    12-09-90  12:00p
 Selected         C          ADDRESS   .WDB      4,858    09-30-89  10:00a
   Number:       1           AMORTIZE  .XLS     11,559    12-09-90  12:00p
   Size  :     202           AMT       .TPR      4,448    09-04-90   4:07p
 Directory                   ANSI      .SYS      9,029    04-09-91   5:00a
   Name : DOS                ANSI31    .HCH         32    04-12-87   2:35p
   Size :   2,332,524        ANSI32    .HCH         63    04-12-87   2:37p
   Files:          96        ANSI33    .HCH         61    04-12-87   2:39p
 Disk                        ANSI37    .HCH         60    04-12-87   2:44p
   Name : JJ                 ANTCOAST  .DAT    184,140    06-23-90   2:13p
   Size :  64,804,864        ANTISLND  .DAT      8,464    06-23-90   1:55p
   Avail:  15,329,280        APERTURE  .XLS      2,666    12-09-90  12:00p
   Files:       1,573        APOGEE    .BAK      2,048    03-20-91   9:17a
   Dirs :          97        APOGEE    .DOC      2,048    03-20-91   9:26a
                             APPEALS   .STY      1,024    10-04-90   3:22p
 F10=Actions  Shift+F9=Command Prompt                              11:35a
```

FIGURE 10-3. *All Files view.*

If you choose Program/File Lists view, your screen display is similar to Figure 10-4. This view shows the Directory Tree, the File list, the Program list, and the Active Task List. When you install the Shell, you are in Program/File Lists view.

If you choose Program List, your screen display is similar to Figure 10-5. Use this view when you are not performing file management tasks. It shows only program groups and items and the Active Task List.

If the screen fails to update itself when you change the view, press F5 or choose Refresh from the View menu.

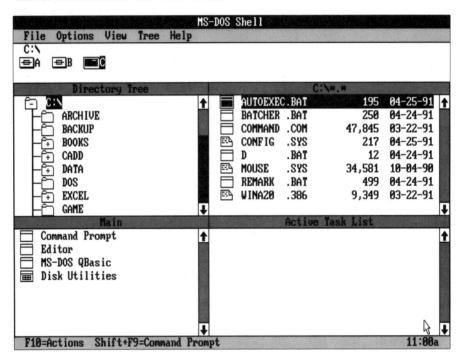

FIGURE 10-4. *Program/File Lists view.*

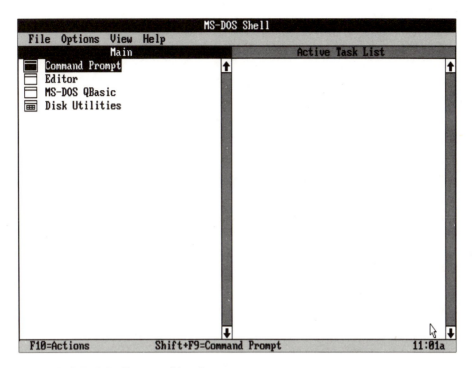

FIGURE 10-5. *Program List view.*

CUSTOMIZING FROM THE COMMAND PROMPT

As discussed in Chapter 6, some features of your system can be controlled only from the command prompt. For an example, see Chapter 6 for instructions on setting the date and the time.

The PROMPT Command

When you install the Shell, the Setup program creates a command prompt to indicate the current directory, followed by a greater-than sign (>), by modifying your AUTOEXEC.BAT file. To see this, use the Editor to open AUTOEXEC.BAT. Look for the following line:

```
prompt $p$g
```

This command causes the prompt to display the current drive and directory, followed by the greater-than sign. If you do not see a line beginning with the PROMPT command, your computer is using the default command prompt.

You can change the command prompt so that it includes any text and the following special characters:

Character	Displayed as
q	Equal sign (=)
$	Dollar sign ($)
t	Current time
d	Current date
p	Current drive and path
v	Version of DOS
n	Current drive
g	Greater-than sign (>)
l	Less-than sign (<)
b	Pipe (¦)

NOTE: The special characters are used with the PROMPT command to produce certain results. For example, if you simply type the greater-than sign with the PROMPT command, DOS interprets it as a redirection instruction rather than as text; to have the greater-than sign displayed in the prompt, you must use the special character g. When you use one of these characters, you must precede it with a dollar sign ($g, for instance) to indicate that it is a special character, not simply text. You can type the letters that represent special characters in either uppercase or lowercase.

For more information on what you can include in the command prompt, see your DOS manual.

Chapter 10: Customizing Your System

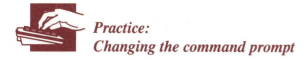
Practice:
Changing the command prompt

1. At the command prompt, type:

   PROMPT $P Your Wish Is My Command$G

   Be sure to include a space before typing *Your*.

2. Press Enter. The command prompt should now look like the following:

   C:\ Your Wish Is My Command>

3. To return to the original prompt, type:

   PROMPT PG

   and press Enter.

If you change your prompt, the change remains in effect until you reboot your computer. When you reboot, the command prompt reverts to the prompt specified in your AUTOEXEC.BAT file. To change your command prompt permanently, change the line in your AUTOEXEC.BAT file and reboot your computer.

 If you are running the Shell and change the command prompt by choosing Command Prompt from the Main program group, the change is in effect until you return to the Shell. If you change the prompt before starting the Shell, the change remains until you reboot or turn off the computer.

CONFIGURING THE OPERATING SYSTEM

When you install DOS 5, two special files are also installed in the root directory of the boot drive: AUTOEXEC.BAT and CONFIG.SYS. At installation time, simple copies of these files are installed. If necessary, you can change them with the Editor.

Because AUTOEXEC.BAT is executed each time you start your computer, you can include in AUTOEXEC.BAT any command that you want to have carried out at that time.

143

CONFIG.SYS contains information about system device drivers—the software for peripherals such as a mouse, a CD ROM drive, or extended memory. If you keep this information in CONFIG.SYS, you can easily update it when you add new peripherals.

Now let's look at some specific tasks you can do with AUTOEXEC.BAT and CONFIG.SYS.

CAUTION: Changing an AUTOEXEC.BAT or CONFIG.SYS file can seriously affect how your computer runs. Always make backup copies of these files before changing the files in any way. You should also have a copy of these files on a bootable floppy disk in case your changes prevent the computer from starting from the hard disk.

Defining the Path

When you type a command or a program name at the command prompt, DOS first looks within itself to see if the program exists. For example, the DIR command is internal to DOS. If the command or program name is not internal to DOS, DOS then looks for it in the current directory—first with a .COM extension, then with a .EXE extension, and finally with a .BAT extension. If it finds none of these, you get an error message telling you that the command or filename can't be found.

To simplify finding and loading, DOS includes a PATH command. You use this command to tell DOS where to look for commands and filenames. In your AUTOEXEC.BAT file is a line similar to the following:

```
PATH C:\DOS
```

This command tells DOS that if a command or a filename is not found in the current directory, DOS is to look in the DOS directory. You should edit this command to include all the program directories you normally use, as shown in this example:

```
PATH C:\WIN;C:\DOS;C:\WP;C:\BAT;C:\UTIL;C:\DBASE
```

Notice that all pathnames are separated by semicolons. DOS now searches for commands or filenames in the order specified in the path.

NOTE: The PATH command works only for programs and batch files (files with .COM, .EXE, or .BAT extensions). DOS cannot use this command to find data files.

To locate files faster, list your most frequently used directories first in the PATH command. DOS looks first for a file in the first listed directory and then in the second one and so on until the file is found.

Defining the Environment

DOS reserves a special area of memory for some global definitions that can be used by any program running under DOS. This memory area is called the environment. You use the SET command to change variables in this area.

For example, many programs write temporary files that are erased when you exit the program. When you install DOS 5, you also install a TEMP subdirectory. DOS stores temporary files in this directory. Look for the following line in your AUTOEXEC.BAT file:

```
SET TEMP=C:\TEMP
```

You can always delete any files in this directory. For example, if a program terminates unexpectedly, check your TEMP subdirectory for temporary files and erase them.

CAUTION: Never delete files from the TEMP subdirectory when any program is running. Doing so can cause loss of data. Be especially careful about deleting temporary files when the Task Swapper is enabled.

As you install more programs, you will probably add more SET commands for more global variables. You might then get a message telling you that you are out of environment space. To create more space, add the following line to the CONFIG.SYS file:

```
SHELL=COMMAND.COM /e:512 /p
```

Be sure not to add space before or after the equal sign. Reboot your computer after adding this line.

Setting Up File Buffers

Another important aspect of customizing your system is specifying how many files will be open at a time and how many buffers are used. Buffers are special memory areas that DOS uses to transfer data to or from files. The safest strategy is to use the values for the most demanding program—often a database manager. You change or set these values in CONFIG.SYS. The two lines might look like this:

```
FILES=40
BUFFERS=15
```

If you use a disk cache (discussed in the following section), the BUFFERS value can be lower.

NOTE: Many programs alter the FILES and BUFFERS lines of the CONFIG.SYS file when the programs are first installed. Decreasing the values on these lines can cause the programs to work erratically—or not at all.

Speeding Up Disk Access

Disk access is slow compared with memory access. To keep your computer working at maximum speed, you can use a disk cache and FASTOPEN.

Using a disk cache

A disk cache is a memory area that holds data being moved to or from the disk. Although the disk cache program itself uses memory, most users find it worth the cost.

DOS 5 includes a disk cache. Install it if you have extended or expanded memory. To do so, add the following line to the CONFIG.SYS file:

```
DEVICE=SMARTDRIVE.SYS 1024 256
```

Remember: No spaces before or after the equal sign.

The first number is the initial cache size in kilobytes. The second number is the minimum cache size in kilobytes. Be sure you have enough physical memory for what you request. If you don't have extended or expanded memory, don't install the cache.

NOTE: The command line for the disk cache must be placed after the command line that controls the extended or expanded memory in the CONFIG.SYS file.

Using FASTOPEN

FASTOPEN is a DOS 5 utility that speeds disk access by creating a cache for certain directory information. To install FASTOPEN, add this line to your CONFIG.SYS file:

    INSTALL=C:\DOS\FASTOPEN.EXE C: 10

The drive designator defines which drive to cache, and the numeral shows the maximum number of files that can be worked on at one time. You should use one file for every megabyte of memory on the drive being cached.

 NOTE: FASTOPEN can be installed from either the AUTOEXEC.BAT file or the CONFIG.SYS file. Check both files before adding FASTOPEN to the CONFIG.SYS file.

TIPS ON CUSTOMIZING YOUR SYSTEM

- Changing your view of the Shell does not delete or add directories or files, nor does it change anything about how the Shell functions. It simply changes what the screen displays. If the Task Swapper is enabled when you choose Single File List from the View menu, for example, the Active Task List disappears from view, but the Task Swapper remains enabled.

- You can change the color of individual screen components, the text of Help messages, and even the number of parameters that can be passed to a program by editing the DOSSHELL.INI file. You must edit this file very carefully, however, or the Shell might not work correctly. Always make a backup of the DOSSHELL.INI file before modifying it in any way.

- When you use the PROMPT command with the $p parameter, the computer must check the disk to determine the current path. If you want your computer to work at maximum speed, you can omit the $p parameter.

- If you run out of memory when running a program, or if the program becomes very slow, try deleting FASTOPEN from your CONFIG.SYS file and then rebooting the computer. This will free more memory for your program.

- You can use a RAMdisk to simulate a disk with memory and decrease the time it takes your computer to read and write information. A RAMdisk is best used for the temporary files normally placed in C:\TEMP. If you have a RAMdisk, and if you have adequate memory to run your application, install the TEMP directory to the RAMdisk instead. If you use Microsoft Windows, however, it's better not to use a RAMdisk and instead to let Windows use all available memory.

Appendixes

Appendix A

Installing DOS 5

If your computer system is new and if you have a hard disk, DOS is probably already installed on your hard disk. If the command prompt or the DOS Shell appears when you start your computer, DOS is already installed. To verify that the correct version has been installed, type *VER* at the command prompt and press Enter.

DOS 5 can be installed on a disk that does not contain any DOS files, or it can be installed as an upgrade from a previous version of DOS. If your computer does not boot, or if you have a version of DOS earlier than 2.11, you must install a new copy of DOS 5, rather than simply upgrading to DOS 5. To install DOS 5 for the first time, you need a set of disks different from those used for an upgrade. Check the documentation that came with your disks or see your computer dealer to be sure you have the correct set.

INSTALLING DOS 5 ON A HARD DISK FOR THE FIRST TIME

If your new computer system includes a hard disk but does not yet have DOS installed, follow these instructions to install DOS 5 for the first time:

1. Have the DOS 5 installation disks ready and arranged in numeric order.
2. Place Disk 1 in drive A.
3. Start your computer.

4. At the A:\> prompt, type:

    SETUP

    and press Enter. Then follow the instructions on the screen.

During the installation process, you are prompted to verify or provide information and to make some choices. If you are a new user of DOS, accept the options that the Setup program proposes; DOS has determined that these are the best choices for your particular system. If you want more information about any of the proposed responses, press F1 for help.

You might need to modify your AUTOEXEC.BAT or CONFIG.SYS file to customize or optimize the operation of your system with DOS 5. If the Setup program placed the word REM before any commands in these files, it was unable to recognize the commands. Your DOS manual will help you determine how to change these lines.

UPGRADING TO DOS 5 ON A HARD DISK

If your computer system includes a hard disk and if you are already running DOS version 2.11 or later, follow these instructions to upgrade to DOS 5:

1. Have the upgrade disks ready and arranged in numeric order. Also have on hand two blank floppy disks.

2. Start your computer.

3. Place Disk 1 in drive A.

4. At the C:\> prompt, type:

    A:SETUP

    and press Enter. Then follow the instructions on the screen.

Before the installation starts, you are asked whether you want to back up your hard disk. This backup procedure is a new safety feature of DOS 5 (as is a built-in recovery program). For more information on backup and recovery, see your DOS manual.

When the installation is complete, label the Recovery disk you made during the installation, and store it in a safe place. If for any reason you need to restore your old version of DOS, place the Recovery disk in drive A and restart the system.

The Setup program also creates a new directory called OLD_DOS.1 (or OLD_DOS.2, if DOS 5 was previously installed) that contains all the DOS files that were on the disk before this installation. After you use your computer with DOS 5 for a while and are sure that you will not need to restore the earlier version of DOS files, you can delete the OLD_DOS.1 directory. Use the DELOLDOS command to delete the files and directory and free the disk space for other uses.

 NOTE: To install DOS 5 on a hard disk, your system must have at least 512 KB of memory and at least 2.8 MB of free disk space. If you need help or information at any time while running the Setup program, press F1.

INSTALLING OR UPGRADING ON A FLOPPY DISK

You can also install DOS 5 or upgrade from an earlier version of DOS on a floppy-disk system. The procedure is similar to that used with a hard-disk system. You will need several blank floppy disks for the installation. To start the procedure, type:

SETUP /F

at the A:\> prompt, press Enter, and follow the instructions on the screen.

 NOTE: Use this procedure only if your computer system does not have a hard disk. If you want to make a backup boot disk for your hard disk, use the FORMAT command (with the /s parameter) and the COPY command to create the boot disk. (See Chapter 3 for details.)

Appendix B

Glossary

Alternate key
A key labeled Alt that, when pressed in combination with another key, gives the other key an alternative meaning. In DOS, Alt is often used with keys on the numeric keyboard to enter ASCII codes for special characters. In the DOS Shell and various applications, Alt is used to access the menu bar.

application program
A computer program—for example, a word processor or a spreadsheet—that performs a specific task.

archive
As a verb, to store copies of files to ensure that the files are not lost. As an adjective, *archive* is a file attribute indicating whether a file has changed since the last time it was backed up.

ASCII
An acronym for American Standard Code for Information Interchange, a numeric code for characters.

attributes
Information stored in the file directory concerning the status or characteristics of a file. Attributes designate a file as hidden, system, archive, or read-only.

AUTOEXEC.BAT
   A special-purpose batch file (set of commands) carried out by DOS when the computer is started or restarted. In DOS 5, the AUTOEXEC.BAT file is created or altered when the system is installed.

backup (back up)
   As a noun, a copy of a program, a disk, or data, made either for archiving purposes or for safeguarding valuable files. As a verb, *back up* means to make a backup copy.

.BAK
   A filename extension indicating that the file contains the second-most-recent version of a file.

Basic
   A programming language included with DOS. DOS 5 features QBasic, a modern version of Basic.

batch file
   A text file that contains a sequence of DOS commands. Its filename extension is .BAT.

bit
   Short for binary digit; either 1 or 0 in the binary number system. A bit is the smallest unit of information handled by a computer.

boot
   As a verb, to start a computer. As a noun, a *boot* is the process of starting or restarting a computer.

byte
   A unit of information consisting of 8 bits; in computer processing and storage, the equivalent of a single character, such as a letter, a numeral, or a punctuation mark.

CGA

An acronym for Color/Graphics Adapter, a video display adapter introduced by IBM in 1981. It shows both text and graphics at low resolution in as many as 16 colors.

cluster

A unit used in disk storage, consisting of a fixed number of sectors. The number of sectors differs depending on the hardware.

command

An instruction to a computer program that, when issued by the user, causes a certain action to be carried out. Commands can be typed at the keyboard or chosen from a menu with either the keyboard or the mouse.

command prompt

Displayed text indicating that a computer program is waiting for a command from the user.

CONFIG.SYS

A special-purpose text file read by DOS when the computer is started or restarted. The CONFIG.SYS file identifies and sets the limits of parameters used by DOS.

Control key

A key labeled Ctrl that, when pressed in combination with another key, gives the other key an alternative meaning. In DOS, Ctrl is often used to issue special control codes for file, screen, and printer control.

current directory

The directory that DOS searches first for a requested file, and the directory in which a new file is stored unless another directory is specified.

current drive

The drive containing the disk that DOS searches first for a requested file, and the drive on which a new file is stored unless another drive is specified.

cursor
>An indicator on the screen that shows where the next character will be displayed. The cursor usually appears as a blinking underline, a rectangle, or a vertical bar.

data
>Items of information stored in a file.

device
>Any computer subsystem—for example, a printer, a disk drive, or a mouse.

dialog box
>An area displayed on the screen of an application, allowing the user to choose options for executing a command or to confirm an action.

directory
>A catalog for filenames and other directories stored on a disk. The topmost directory is called the root directory; the directories within a directory are called subdirectories.

disk
>A round, flat piece of flexible plastic (floppy disk) or inflexible metal (hard disk) coated with a magnetic material that can be electrically influenced to hold information recorded in digital (binary) form. In most computers, a disk is the primary means of storing data on a permanent or semipermanent basis.

disk drive
>An electromechanical device that reads from and writes to disks. The two types of disk drives in common use are floppy-disk drives and hard-disk drives.

diskette
>*See* floppy disk.

display
>The visual output of a computer.

Appendix B: Glossary

Doskey
In DOS 5, a program that records commands and enables you to repeat, edit, or store them as batch files or keyboard macros.

edit
As a verb, to change the contents of a file. As a noun, Edit is the name of the command that starts the MS-DOS Editor, the menu-based text editor included with DOS 5.

editor
A program used to create or change text files.

EGA
An acronym for Enhanced Graphics Adapter, a video display adapter introduced by IBM in 1984. It shows both text and graphics at medium resolution in as many as 64 colors.

extension
A set of as many as three characters added to a filename that identifies the contents of the file more precisely. The extension .DOC, for example, indicates a document file.

file
A complete, named collection of information, such as a program, a set of data used by a program, or a user-created document. A file is the basic unit of storage that enables a computer to distinguish one set of information from another.

filename
The set of letters, numbers, and allowable symbols assigned to a file that distinguishes it from all other files in a particular directory on a disk. In DOS, a filename can include as many as eight characters and, in addition to alphanumeric characters, can include certain punctuation marks, such as hyphens and underlines.

fixed disk
See hard disk.

floppy disk
    A round, flat piece of Mylar coated with ferric oxide and encased in a protective plastic cover, the disk jacket or disk shell. Data is stored on a floppy disk by the disk drive's head, which alters the magnetic orientation of the particles.

format
    A process performed by the computer's operating system or a utility program that organizes the storage space on the disk so that it becomes, in essence, a collection of data "compartments," each capable of being located by the operating system.

hard disk
    One or more inflexible platters coated with material that allows the magnetic recording of computer data. A hard disk is sealed to prevent contaminants from interfering with the close head-to-disk tolerances. Compared to floppy disks, hard disks provide faster access to data and can store much more information.

hardware
    The physical components of a computer system, including any peripheral equipment such as printers, modems, and mice.

hexadecimal
    The base-16 number system that consists of the digits 0 through 9 and the uppercase or lowercase letters A (equivalent to decimal 10) through F (equivalent to decimal 15). Hexadecimal, usually called hex, is commonly used in programming as a compact means of representing the binary numbers of a byte used internally by a computer.

hidden
    An attribute that prevents a file from being shown in the normal listing of a directory. Files are hidden to protect them from change or deletion. DOS, for example, contains two hidden files; both contain critical portions of the operating system.

initialize
> *See* format.

MCGA
> An acronym for Multi-Color Graphics Array, a video display adapter included in the IBM PS/2 Models 25 and 30. It shows both text and graphics at low to medium resolution in as many as 256 colors.

MDA
> An acronym for Monochrome Display Adapter, a video display adapter introduced in 1981. It shows text only, not graphics, at medium resolution in one color.

memory
> An area that stores information electronically. The term *memory* can refer to RAM, ROM, or disk drives, but in common usage it usually refers only to RAM.

menu
> A list of options from which the user chooses an item. In many applications, a menu is accessed from a menu bar, and a command is then chosen from the menu.

operating system
> The software responsible for controlling the allocation and usage of hardware resources such as memory, central processing unit (CPU) time, disk space, and peripheral devices. The operating system is the foundation on which applications, such as word processing and spreadsheet programs, are built.

parallel port
> A communications device that is usually connected to a parallel printer. A computer can have more than one parallel port; the first port is labeled LPT1, the second LPT2, and so on.

parameter
> A qualifier included with a command to define more specifically what the command is to do. Arguments and switches are types of parameters.

path
> The sequence of directory names that defines the location of a directory or a file.

pathname
> The portion of a file specification that defines the path to the file. It can include a drive letter followed by a colon.

pipe (|)
> A portion of memory that can be used by one process to pass information along to another. On your keyboard, it is typed by pressing Shift+\ (holding down Shift while you press the backslash key).

program
> A set of instructions for a computer.

prompt
> Displayed text indicating that a computer program is waiting for input from the user.

RAM
> An acronym for random access memory, the hardware of a computer where information can be temporarily stored and retrieved. The first 640 KB of RAM is considered conventional memory, and the next 384 KB is reserved memory. Any additional memory is extended or expanded memory.

read-only
> An attribute that allows a file to be read but not changed. A read-only file that has been changed can be saved using a different filename.

ROM
> An acronym for read-only memory, hardware containing information that can be read but unable to store any additional information.

root directory
> The main directory that DOS creates on each disk; the top directory in a multilevel filing system.

serial port

A communications device that is usually connected to a modem or a serial printer. A computer can have more than one serial port; the first port is labeled COM1, the second COM2, and so on.

shell

A computer program that creates an easy-to-use interface for the user and then passes commands to a different program to be carried out. It is called a shell because it effectively surrounds the other program, hiding it from view.

software

Computer programs; instructions that cause the hardware—the machines—to do work. The primary kinds of software are operating systems and application programs.

subdirectory

A directory within another directory.

system

A file attribute indicating that the file is to provide information to DOS. Such files usually have filenames with the .SYS extension.

text

Data that consists of characters representing the words and symbols of human speech. Text is one form in which computers can store and transmit information.

VGA

An acronym for Video Graphics Array, a video display adapter introduced by IBM in 1987. It shows both text and graphics at medium to high resolution in as many as 256 colors.

volume label

A name for a disk, usually assigned by the user when the disk is formatted.

wildcard character
   A special character, like a wildcard in a poker game, that can be used to represent any other character. In DOS, the two wildcard characters are the question mark (?) and the asterisk (*).

write-protected
   Describes a floppy disk whose write-protect notch is closed, thus preventing data from being written to that disk.

Appendix C

Keyboard and Mouse Conventions

KEYBOARD

Key(s)	Result
F1	Gets HELP
F3	Exits Shell
F5	Rereads directories on current disk
F7	Moves selected file
F8	Copies selected file
F9	Views contents of selected file
F9 (within View File Contents)	Toggles View display between ASCII and hex
F10	Toggles menu bar
Alt+F4	Exits Shell
Shift+F5	Repaints screen
Shift+F8	Toggles add mode for discontinuous file selection
Shift+F9	Goes to the command prompt without exiting Shell
Ctrl+Home	Moves to start of list
Ctrl+End	Moves to end of list

(continued)

Key(s)	Result
Ctrl+Esc	Returns to Shell from task (application program)
Ctrl+*drive*	Switches to *drive*
Ctrl+/ (slash)	Selects all files
Ctrl+\ (backslash)	Cancels all selections
Ctrl+∗ (asterisk)	Expands all branches of Directory Tree
+ (plus)	Expands selected branch of Directory Tree to next level
− (minus)	Collapses an entire branch of Directory Tree
∗ (asterisk)	Expands selected branch of Directory Tree to all levels
Alt	Toggles menu bar
End	Moves to end of current line
Enter	Initiates action
Esc	Cancels command or closes dialog box
Home	Moves to start of current line
Spacebar (choosing commands)	Executes selected command button
Spacebar (selecting options)	Toggles selection of option
Spacebar (add mode)	Toggles selection of file
Shift+Spacebar (add mode)	Selects all files between selected file and cursor
Tab	Moves forward (or clockwise) one field
letter	Moves to next selection that starts with *letter*
Up arrow	Moves cursor up one line
Down arrow	Moves cursor down one line
Left arrow	Moves cursor left one character
Right arrow	Moves cursor right one character
PgUp	Scrolls one screen toward top
PgDn	Scrolls one screen toward bottom

(continued)

Key(s)	Result
Shift+Tab	Moves backward one field
Shift+Up arrow	Moves selected list of files upward by one item
Shift+Down arrow	Moves selected list of files downward by one item
Shift+Alt+Esc	Transfers control to previous application in Active Task List or to Shell if current application is at top of Active Task List
Alt+Esc	Transfers control to next application in Active Task List or to Shell if current application is at bottom of Active Task List
Alt+Tab	Displays, in turn, title bar of each active application, including Shell (control transferred to listed application when keys released)

MOUSE

Mouse Action	Result
Click	Deselects all and then selects item under mouse pointer
Double-click	Initiates action using selected item
Drag-and-release	Moves selected file(s) to another directory or drive
Ctrl+drag-and-release	Copies selected file(s) to another directory or drive
Ctrl+click	Toggles selection of file under mouse pointer without affecting other selected files
Shift+drag	Makes continuous file selection

Appendix D

Troubleshooting

This appendix presents some common problems you might encounter when you use DOS 5 and the DOS Shell—and it also offers some possible solutions. See your DOS manual and the README.TXT file that comes on the DOS disks for information about problems not discussed here.

GENERAL PROBLEMS

I modified the AUTOEXEC.BAT file or the CONFIG.SYS file, but the changes didn't "take."

Reboot the computer. Changes to these files won't take until you reboot. During the reboot, watch the screen for any error messages, and modify the file accordingly.

I set the time and date, but each time I reboot, the changes are lost.

If you are using a PC/XT or an XT clone, you need a clock card to maintain date and time information when the computer is turned off. If you have a clock card or are using a PC/AT or later type of IBM computer, losing date and time changes indicates that the clock battery is dead. Replace the battery.

The system won't boot.

Be sure that all the computer's cables are connected and that all the system's components are turned on. Try to boot from your bootable floppy disk, and then switch to the hard disk and read it. (A simple way to do this is with the DIR command.) If you can read the hard disk, restore DOS to it by copying the DOS system files from the boot floppy. At the A:\> prompt, type *SYS C:* and press Enter. If you have recently modified the CONFIG.SYS or the AUTOEXEC.BAT file, replace the modified version of the file with the backup version. You should now be able to boot from the hard disk.

If you can't read the hard disk, you might have problems with the disk controller or with the hard disk itself. If you can't read the floppy disk, you have some other kind of hardware problem. Run your system diagnostics, or take your computer to be repaired.

DOS ERROR MESSAGES

`Bad command or file name`

The command or file is not in the current directory or path. Check your spelling and typing for errors, and be sure you are in the right directory.

`Cannot load COMMAND, system halted`

DOS can't find the command interpreter in the current directory. If a PATH command is active, DOS can't find it in any directory of the path. If the SHELL command has been added to CONFIG.SYS, DOS can't find COMMAND.COM in the directory specified by this command.

`Duplicate filename or file not found`

When you tried to rename a file, either you gave it the name of a file already on the disk or DOS could not find the file to rename. Check the spelling of the filename and the existing entries in the current directory.

`File cannot be copied onto itself`

You tried to use a COPY command to copy a file to the directory in which it already exists. Include the full path of the destination in the command. To make a copy of the file in the same directory, you must change the filename.

Appendix D: Troubleshooting

Syntax error

You entered a command incorrectly. Check the command syntax in your DOS manual or the manual for the program you are using.

Incorrect DOS version

You are using a DOS command that does not exist in the version of DOS installed on your system. If you are using DOS 5, be sure that the program being read is compatible with DOS 5. Trying to use the Shell with an old version of DOS or using older commands in DOS 5 can produce this message.

ABORT, RETRY, FAIL

This message typically follows another message line. The first line is usually self-explanatory, telling you that the computer cannot use a device or cannot carry out an operation. For example, you might see this message if you try to print a file when your printer is not ready.

If you get this message when you are using a floppy disk, first be sure that the disk is not write-protected and that the disk drive door is closed. Also be sure that the disk is formatted—DOS can't use unformatted disks. Format the disk in the drive for which you intend to use it; that is, don't format a low-density disk in a high-capacity drive unless the specific low-density formatting switches have been set. If you get this message when the disk drive door is closed and the disk is formatted and not write-protected, the disk might be physically damaged. Try another disk. If it doesn't read, the disk drive might be malfunctioning. If the second disk reads, return to the defective disk. Salvage the information (if you can), and then reformat the disk. If you get the ABORT, RETRY, FAIL message when formatting a disk, throw the disk away.

If this message occurs with a hard-disk system, you might have hardware problems. Try to reboot from a floppy disk, and then try to read the hard disk.

Insufficient disk space

The current disk or the root directory is full. Remove files to release some space. Filenames and subdirectory entries require space in the root directory; deleting either can free up space in that directory.

```
Non-System disk or disk error
Replace and strike any key when ready
```
> You tried to boot from a disk that does not have DOS installed on it. This message is common if you have a floppy disk in a drive when the computer is first turned on. Remove the floppy (or substitute one that has DOS installed on it), and press Enter. The computer will reboot.

SHELL PROBLEMS

In general, the Shell's error messages are usually similar to DOS error messages, although the Shell messages often allow you to take immediate corrective action. Follow the instructions on the screen to remedy the problem, or press F1 for Help.

Some common problems you might encounter when using the Shell are described below.

The Editor will not run.

> Be sure that both the EDIT.COM and the QBASIC.EXE files are either in the current directory or in a directory listed in the PATH command. The Editor will not run without the QBasic program.

A file will not print, or the printer prints strange characters.

> The file you are trying to print is probably not a text file. Use the View File Contents command from the File menu to check the contents of the file. If the file is shown in hexadecimal numbers, for example, it is not a text file and should not be printed. If the file is an application data file, start the application, and then print the file from the application. If you cannot print a text file from the Shell or the Editor, save the file, return to the Shell, and run the PRINT.EXE program. This will allow you to return to the Editor and print the text.

Everything slows down, and your work is interrupted by long pauses.

> You might be running out of memory, or you might be running other programs in the background. If you have used the Print command and the printing is not yet completed, the print queue might still be active. When the printing is completed, the computer should return to its normal

working speed. If you are using the Task Swapper, close the applications you are not using. You might also want to disable the Task Swapper. If you are using an application that creates a data file, save the data file frequently. You can adjust the BUFFER value in the CONFIG.SYS file to decrease the number of times the application writes to a temporary file. It's also possible that you are running multiple copies of the Shell or COMMAND.COM.

Your computer doesn't seem to have enough memory to run a program.

Check the program's documentation to see how much memory is required to run the program, and verify that your computer has sufficient memory. If the program requires most of the computer's memory, exit the Shell and run the program from the command prompt. Also be sure that memory-resident programs are not running. (FASTOPEN and Mirror, for example, are two memory-resident programs that come with DOS.) You might need to reboot the computer to clear the memory. You should also be sure that the Task Swapper is disabled.

If you suddenly start to run out of memory with programs that ran well in earlier sessions, you might have multiple copies of the Shell or other programs loaded into memory. This can occur, for example, when you run the command prompt from the Shell and then load another copy of the Shell rather than exiting back to the Shell—that is, you type *DOSSHELL* instead of *EXIT* to return to the Shell. To delete extra copies of programs, quit any applications that are running, and quit the Shell by choosing Exit from the File menu. Then, at the command prompt, type *EXIT* and press Enter. If nothing happens, no extra copies are in memory. But if you see another application, or if the Shell reappears, extra copies are running. Continue exiting the applications or the Shell and typing *EXIT* at the command prompt until nothing happens. You can then restart the Shell or the application with more available memory. Remember to type *EXIT* to return to the Shell whenever you run Command Prompt from the Main program group.

You highlight a command, a file, or a program, but nothing happens.

You have selected the item but have not chosen it. To carry out the selected command or run the selected program, press Enter or double-click the item with the mouse. You can also use certain function keys to carry out commands.

If you choose a command from a menu and nothing happens, that command might be unavailable. Remove the highlight from the command, and check the command's appearance. If it differs from that of other commands (the name is lighter or grayed, for example), the Shell is preventing you from executing an inappropriate command by making the command unavailable. Be sure that the appropriate area of the Shell window is active before you choose the command again.

PRINTER PROBLEMS

The computer times out, saying that the printer is not ready.

Check to ensure that the printer is on and ready to print. (Most printers have a "ready" or "online" light.) Be sure that the cable to the printer is connected firmly at each end. Parallel printers should connect to LPT1 or the parallel printer port; serial printers should connect to COM1, COM2, or the serial printer port. You might need to use the MODE command to redirect the output to the correct port.

The computer stalls when printing.

Some serial printers stall if the printer is not ready or if the port is not configured properly. Check the cable, be sure that the printer is ready (and has paper), and reissue a MODE command for the correct configuration if necessary.

The printer does not print the proper characters.

If you are using a serial printer, be sure that the MODE command was issued correctly. Check to see that the switches on the printer are set correctly for this mode and that the cable is connected properly and firmly. If a unique font has been downloaded to the printer, attempt to download it again.

Graphics characters don't print correctly.

If you are using a laser printer, be sure that the proper font is selected at the printer. Some fonts don't have a graphics extension. A Courier font, for example, can be stored in several variations, only one of which has the graphics extension. Run a test print using the printer's test mode to get a font listing, and identify a font with a graphics extension. Then select that font.

If you are using a dot-matrix printer, it must be set to the correct mode. Some printers, for example, run in either Epson or IBM mode and can print the IBM extended character set only in IBM mode. You might need to reset the printer's DIP switches to change modes. Some printers, however, cannot print any of the graphics characters in the IBM extended character set.

Appendix E

Recommended Reading

This book has covered the basics of DOS and the DOS Shell. But there's a lot more to learn about DOS: How do the various versions of DOS differ? How can you customize DOS to work the way you work? How can you make DOS take advantage of the extra memory in your computer? How can you start writing DOS programs? The following books are recommended to help you find the answers.

Wolverton, Van. *Running MS-DOS, 5th Edition.* Redmond, Washington: Microsoft Press, 1991.

> A general introduction to personal computers and the MS-DOS operating system. Covers MS-DOS versions 3.1 through 5.0. Highly recommended for those interested in learning more about DOS commands and writing batch files.

Wolverton, Van, and Dan Gookin. *Supercharging MS-DOS, 3d Edition.* Redmond, Washington: Microsoft Press, 1991.

> The official power user's guide to customizing an MS-DOS computer with DOS commands, batch files, and debug scripts. Covers editing CONFIG.SYS and AUTOEXEC.BAT files, using a RAMdisk, managing extended and expanded memory, configuring HP LaserJet and Epson printers, and configuring DOS for use with Microsoft Windows.

Gookin, Dan. *The Microsoft Guide to Managing Memory with MS-DOS 5*. Redmond, Washington: Microsoft Press, 1991.

> An interesting and in-depth look at DOS memory management. Covers buying and installing memory; configuring conventional, extended, and expanded memory; using a RAMdisk; and using memory efficiently with application programs and Microsoft Windows.

Jamsa, Kris. *MS-DOS Batch Files, 2d Edition: Microsoft Quick Reference*. Redmond, Washington: Microsoft Press, 1991.

> An introduction and reference to customizing your computer with batch files. Updated for DOS 5.

Wolverton, Van. *MS-DOS, 5th Edition: Microsoft Quick Reference*. Redmond, Washington: Microsoft Press, 1991.

> A handy quick reference to every DOS command. Updated for DOS 5.

Wolverton, Van. *Hard Disk Management, 3d Edition: Microsoft Quick Reference*. Redmond, Washington: Microsoft Press, 1991.

> A pocket guide to managing your hard disk with DOS 5. Includes information about configuring DOS for your system, formatting your hard disk, organizing files and directories, and doing periodic backups.

Halvorson, Michael, and David Rygmyr. *Running MS-DOS QBasic*. Redmond, Washington: Microsoft Press, 1991.

> An introduction to writing DOS application programs with the Basic programming language that comes with DOS 5. Designed for readers with no previous programming experience. Includes questions and programming exercises.

Microsoft Corporation. *Learning DOS*. Redmond, Washington: Microsoft Corporation, 1991.

> A computer-based training (CBT) software package that helps you learn DOS commands and operations. Highly recommended for those who want to learn about using a computer from a computer.

Stinson, Craig, and Nancy Andrews. *Running Windows, 2d Edition.* Redmond, Washington: Microsoft Press, 1990.

A complete introduction and reference to Microsoft Windows version 3.0—the graphical interface that everyone's talking about. Moving to Microsoft Windows is the next logical step for those who have mastered the DOS Shell.

Index

Italicized page numbers indicate graphics.

Special Characters

∗ (asterisk)
   as Directory Tree operator 166
   as wildcard character 24–25, 89, 164
+ (plus sign) as Directory Tree operator 52, 166
− (minus sign) as Directory Tree operator 52, 166
- (hyphen) as parameter modifier 85
. (period)
   as current directory symbol 54, 55
   used with filename extension 22
.. (double period) as parent directory symbol 54, 55, 90
… (ellipsis) as dialog box symbol 7, 71
? (question mark) as wildcard character 24–25, 164
@ (at sign) as display suppression operator (batch files) 128
\ (backslash)
   as pathname separator 53
   as root directory symbol 51, 90
| (pipe operator) 92, 162
♦ (diamond) as toggle symbol 7
$ (dollar sign) as PROMPT command operator 142

A

Active Task List 75–76, 137–41, 147
All Files view 139
Alt (Alternate) key 7, 71, 155, 166
Alt+Esc key combination 167
Alt+F4 key combination 17, 81, 165
Alt+Tab key combination 76, 167
antistatic mats 99
applications. *See* programs
archive files 40, 155
arguments. *See* parameters
arrow keys 6, 7, 9, 12, 115, 116, 166
ASCII (American Standard Code for Information Interchange) 26, 155
associating files 66–67
asterisk (∗)
   as Directory Tree operator 166
   as wildcard character 24–25, 89, 164
at sign (@) as display suppression operator (batch files) 128
attributes, file 40, 51, 155, 160, 162, 163
AUTOEXEC.BAT file
   backing up 144
   on bootable floppy disk 43, 144
   CONFIG.SYS and 143–44
   controlling command prompt display 141–43
   installing DOS 5 and 152
   installing FASTOPEN 147
   modifying 92, 169, 170
   and PATH command 53, *54*, 61, 144–45
   setting date and time 94
   setting environment variables 145
   viewing 27

B

backing up. *See also* copying
  batch files for 126–30
  directories 106–7
  floppy disks 103
  hard disks 102–3, 104–7, 152
  procedures 99, 103–7, 109–10
  program disks 45, 101, 102
  restoring from backups 107–8
  strategies 61, 101–3, 109–10
backslash (\)
  as pathname separator 53
  as root directory symbol 51, 90
Backspace key 9, 94, 116
Backup Fixed Disk (Disk Utilities program group) 65, 103, 105–7
.BAK filename extension 23, 156
.BAS filename extension 67
Basic language 156. *See also* MS-DOS QBasic (Main program group)
batch files. *See also* AUTOEXEC.BAT file
  clearing the screen 130
  comments in 128–29
  creating, with Editor 121, 125, 126–27
  directory for 60, 61
  filename extension 32, 53, 123, 130, 131, 144, 145, 156
  GOTO command 130
  naming 123, 131
  overview 95, 123, 125–26, 156
  pause in execution 129–30
  running 127, 131
  suppressing display 127–28
  suspending 131
  terminating 127

.BAT filename extension 32, 53, 123, 130, 131, 144, 145, 156
bootable disks 40, 42–43, 44, 153, 169–70
buffers, file 146
BUFFERS command (DOS) 146
bulletin boards 100
buttons, command 8, 9–10
buttons, option 10–12
bytes
  and clusters 39–40
  defined 21, 156
  and disk sectors 37
  and size of files 21

C

C:\> prompt. *See* command prompt (DOS)
caches, disk 146–47
case of characters 4, 82, 118, 142
CD (Change Directory) command (DOS) 82, 89, 90
characters
  case of 4, 82, 118, 142
  command prompt special 142
  printing graphics 175
  wildcard 24–25, 33, 85, 89, 95, 164
check boxes 10–12
child directories 51, 52
CHKDSK command (DOS) 52–53, 86–88
.CHK filename extension 86–88
choosing
  commands 6, 172–73
  techniques 7, 12, 172–73
CLS command (batch files) 130
clusters, file 39–40, 86, 157
colors, display 12–13, 120, *121*, 133, 135–36

COM1 and COM2 printer ports 174
.COM filename extension 22, 26, 53, 66, 144, 145
command buttons 8, 9–10
command prompt (DOS). *See also* Command Prompt (Main program group); commands
  accessing, from Shell 13, 68, 81
  changing display of 94, 133, 141–43, 147
  changing drives 83
  checking disks 86–88
  controlling scrolling 84–85, 92, 94
  copying files 22, 88, 103
  described 79, 81
  displaying directories 84–85 (*see also* DIR command (DOS))
  editing commands with Doskey 91–92
  formatting disks 43, 93
  getting help 82
  managing directories 89–91
  naming disks 43–44
  printing files 92–93
  renaming files 89
  running batch files 127, 131
  setting date and time 81, 83, 133
  Shell vs. 79, 81, 133
  starting programs 68, 113
  viewing text files 88
Command Prompt (Main program group) 13, 17, 65, 68, 81, 94, 143, 173
commands. *See also* command buttons; *names of specific commands*
  choosing 6–7, 172–73
  editing 91–92, 94

commands, *continued*
  help with 15–16, *16,* 82, 94
  unavailable 174
comments, in batch files 128–29
comparing disks 45–46
COMP command (DOS) 45–46
compression programs, file 103
CONFIG.SYS file
  AUTOEXEC.BAT and 143–44
  backing up 144
  on bootable floppy disk 43, 144
  contents 144
  creating environment space 145
  installing disk caches 146–47
  installing DOS 5 and 152
  installing RAMdisks 148
  modifying 146, 169, 170, 173
  setting file buffers 146, 173
confirmation options 136–37. *See also* Options menu (Shell), Confirmation command
COPY command (DOS) 33, 88, 103, 153, 170
copying. *See also* backing up; COPY command (DOS)
  disks 44–45
  files 22, 30–31, 33, 88, 103
C prompt (C:\>) 79, 81. *See also* command prompt (DOS)
Ctrl (Control) key 23, 30, 71, 157
Ctrl+∗ (asterisk) key combination 166
Ctrl+\ (backslash) key combination 166
Ctrl+/(slash) key combination 24, 166
Ctrl+Alt+Del key combination 43
Ctrl+Break key combination 94, 127
Ctrl+C key combination 94, 105, 127
Ctrl+End key combination 116, 165
Ctrl+Esc key combination 76, 166
Ctrl+Home key combination 116, 165

Ctrl+Left arrow key combination 116
Ctrl+Right arrow key combination 116
Ctrl+S key combination 84, 94
Ctrl+T key combination 116
current directory 52, 54–55, 84, 157. *See also* DIR command (DOS); directories; File list
current drive 83, 157. *See also* drive list; drives
customizing
   changing command prompt display 94, 133, 141–43, 147
   changing Editor program display 120–21
   from command prompt vs. from Shell 133
   configuring systems 143–47
   enabling Task Swapper 74–76, 137
   installing disk caches 146–47
   setting environment variables 145
   setting file buffers 146
   Shell confirmation level 136–37
   Shell display 135–36, 147
   Shell Program list 68–73
   Shell views 137–41
cutting and pasting (Editor) 115, 116, 118

D

data files. *See also* text files (Editor)
   associating, with programs 66–67
   described 22–23
   and PATH command 145
data losses, preventing
   hardware-related 99–100
   software-related 100–101
   user-related 101

DATE command (DOS) 83, 94, 169
dated backups 102
defragmentation utilities 40, 47
Del (Delete) key 8, 9, 25, 33, 58, 59, 73, 115, 116
Delete command. *See* File menu (Shell), Delete command
deleting
   directories 58–59, 89, 91, 136
   files 25, 33, 58, 94, 101, 136
   program items and groups 73
   text 8–9
DELOLDOS command (DOS) 153
deselecting 6, 23
dialog boxes
   command buttons 9–10
   list boxes 12–13
   option buttons and check boxes 10–12
   overview 7–8, 158
   text boxes 8–9
diamond (♦) as toggle symbol 7
differential backups 102
DIP switches 175
DIR command (DOS) 54–55, 84–85, 90, 170
directories. *See also* Directory Tree; root directory
   backing up single 106–7
   changing current 82, 89, 90
   child 51, 52
   creating 56–57, 89, 91
   current 52, 84–85, 157
   deleting 58–59, 89, 91, 136
   displaying 51, 52, 55, 56, 84 (*see also* DIR command (DOS); File list)
   naming 52, 54–55, 57–58, 61
   networks and 60

directories, *continued*
  organizing 51, 59–60, 61
  overview 21, 49, 51–52
  parent 51, 52, 55, 90
  renaming 57–58
  selecting files across 24
  specifying, for programs 52–54, 70, 144–45
  subdirectories 49, 51, 52, 61, 84, 85
  symbols 40, 51, 52, 54, 55, 90
  viewing and hiding 52
Directory Tree 5, 6, 51–53, *51*, 56, *57,* 89
DISKCOMP command (DOS) 46
Disk Copy (Disk Utilities program group) 44–45, 65
DISKCOPY command (DOS) 103
diskettes. *See* floppy disks
disks. *See also* backing up; directories; floppy disks; hard disks
  access speed 40, 47, 60, 146–47
  bootable 40, 42–43, 44, 169–70
  caches 146–47
  capacity 37–39
  checking 52–53, 86–88
  comparing 45–46
  copying 44–45
  file management 39–40
  finding information about 38–39
  formatting 38, 41–43, 47, 65, 93, 94, 160
  handling 47–48, 100
  labeling 47, 102
  naming 42, 43–44, 163
  organization 37–39
  preventing data losses 42, 47–48, 99–101
  RAM 148

disks, *continued*
  recovering 42, 46, 107–8
  types 35, 37–48, 158
  unformatting 42, 46, 94, 109
Disk Utilities program group 13–14, 65. *See also* Backup Fixed Disk; Disk Copy; Format; Quick Format; Restore Fixed Disk; Undelete
Display menu (viewing files) 26
display modes 5, 16–17, 133, 135–36. *See also* graphics mode; text mode
.DOC filename extension 22, 23, 66–67
document files. *See* text files (Editor)
dollar sign ($) as PROMPT command operator 142
DOS (Disk Operating System). *See* MS-DOS version 5
DOS command prompt. *See* command prompt (DOS)
DOS directory 59, 60
Doskey program 91–92, 159
DOSSHELL command (DOS) 3, 13, 17, 81, 94, 173. *See also* Shell program
DOSSHELL.INI file 136, 147
dot-matrix printers 175
double period (..) as parent directory symbol 54, 55, 90
drive list 5
drives
  changing 83
  current 83, 157
  floppy-disk 39, 45, 46, 83
  and formatting 42, 93, 171
Dual File Lists view 138

E

ECHO command (batch files) 127–28
editing text 8, 9, 115–16
Edit menu (Editor)
  Copy command 118
  Cut command 115, 116
  Paste command 115, 116, 118
Editor program
  on Active Task List 75–76
  copying text 118
  creating and editing batch files 121, 125, 126–27
  customizing 120–21
  editing text 115–16
  exiting 113, 120
  managing files 114–18
  overview 13, 65, 70–71, 111, 113, *114*
  printing files 117–18
  QBasic and 172
  screen 113–14, *114*
  searching for and replacing text 111, 118–20
  starting 66–68, 113, 114–15
  word processors vs. 111, 121
ellipsis (...) as dialog box symbol 7, 71
Enable Task Swapper. *See* Options menu (Shell), Enable Task Swapper command
End key 9, 116, 166
Enter key 9, 166
environment variables 145
Epson printer mode 175
error messages (DOS) 170–72
Esc (Escape) key 7, 10, 94, 166
.EXE filename extension 22, 26, 53, 66, 144, 145

EXIT command (DOS) 13, 17, 81, 94, 173
extensions, filename
  batch files 32, 123, 144, 145
  described 22–23
  text files 32
  using 33

F

F1 key 10, 15, 94, 113, 153, 165
F3 key 17, 81, 88, 119, 125, 165
F5 key 140, 165
F7 key 32, 165
F8 key 30–31, 165
F9 key 26, 27, 165
F10 key 7, 165
FASTOPEN 146, 147, 148, 173
FAT (File Allocation Table) 40, 109
File Display Options. *See* Options menu (Shell), File Display Options command
File list
  changing sort order 11–12, 26
  initial 56
  overview 5, 14–15, 21
  running batch files 127
  running programs 14–15, 66–67, 113
  selecting files in 23–25
  views 137–40
File menu (Editor)
  Exit command 115, 120, 125
  Print command 117
  Save command 117, 125, 126, 128
  uses 114
File menu (Shell)
  adding to Program list 68–73
  Associate command 67
  Copy command 30–31

File menu (Shell), *continued*
  Create Directory command 56–57
  Delete command 25, 33, 58, 59, 73
  Deselect All command 23
  Exit command 17, 66
  Move command 32
  New command 69–70, 72
  Open command 14
  Print command 33
  Properties command 70–71
  Rename command 32, 57–58
  Reorder command 73
  Run command 7–8, 45–46, 52–53, 54–55, 67, 77, 113
  running batch files 127, 131
  running programs 10, 45–46, 67
  Search command 29–30, 87–88
  Select All command 24, 58
  View File Contents command 26–27, 88, 172
files. *See also* archive files; attributes, file; backing up; batch files; data files; Editor program; File list; hidden files; programs; read-only files; system files; text files (Editor)
  associating 66–67
  buffers 146
  clusters 39–40, 86, 157
  copying 22, 30–31, 33, 88, 103
  creating 117
  deleting 25, 33, 58, 94, 101, 136
  deselecting 23
  finding 29–30, 87–88 (*see also* pathnames)
  finding information about 27–29
  icons 21
  managing, on a disk 39–40
  moving 31–32

files, *continued*
  naming 22–23, 32, 33, 52, 53, 89, 159
  overview 19, 21
  printing 22, 32–33, 92–93, 117, 118, 172–73
  renaming 22, 32, 88, 89, 170
  saving 22, 117
  selecting 23–25
  temporary 60, 101, 127, 145, 148
  types 22–23
  undeleting 94, 101, 108–9
  viewing contents of 22, 26–27, 88
FILES command (DOS) 146
filters, DOS 92
fixed disks. *See* hard disks
floppy disks
  backing up 103
  capacity 38
  cluster mapping 39–40
  comparing 45–46
  copying 44–45
  determining number of, for backup 104–5
  drives for 39
  formatting 41–43, 93
  handling 47–48
  installing or upgrading DOS 5 on 153
  overview 35, 37
Format (Disk Utilities program group) 41–42, 65
FORMAT command (DOS) 43, 46, 93, 153
formatting disks 38, 41–43, 47, 65, 93, 94, 160
formatting text 111, 121
fragmented files 40
full backups 102, 104–6

187

G

GOTO command (batch files) 130
graphics characters, printing 175
graphics mode 5, 16–17, *17*, 21, 135
groups, program 65, 68, 71–73, 77

H

hard disks
    backing up 102–3, 104–7, 152
    capacity 37, 49
    cluster mapping 39–40
    crashes 97
    formatting 41, 47, 93
    installing DOS 5 on 151–52
    overview 35, 37, 160
    restoring 108
    upgrading DOS 5 on 152–53
hardware-related data losses 99–100
HELP command (DOS) 82, 94
Help command button 10
Help menu (Shell) 15
help with commands 10, 15–16, *16*, 82, 94
hexadecimal code 26, 160, 172
hidden files 40, 44, 84, 85, 160
.HLP filename extension 23
Home key 9, 116, 166
hyphen (-) as parameter modifier 85

I

IBM printer mode 175
icons, file folder 21
incremental backups 102
Ins (Insert) key 116, 117
insert mode 116, 117
installing DOS 5 151–53

K

keyboard. *See also individual key names and key combinations*
    application shortcuts 71
    choosing command buttons 10
    choosing commands 7
    choosing list box items 12
    conventions 165–67
    copying files 30–31
    editing text 9, 116–17
    moving files 32
    selecting and choosing 6
    selecting dialog box options 11–12
    selecting files 24
    selecting text 9

L

LABEL command (DOS) 43–44
labels, volume 42, 43–44, 163
laser printers 175
list boxes 12–13
LPT1 printer port 118, 174

M

magnetic fields 47–48
Main program group. *See also Command Prompt (Main program group); Disk Utilities program group; Editor program; MS-DOS QBasic (Main program group); Program list*
    adding programs 68–73
    overview 13, 65, 73
    starting programs 65, 66, 69, 113
MD (Make Directory) command (DOS) 89, 91

memory
  disk caches 146–47
  displaying information about 10, 15, 86, *87*
  problems 17, 94, 173
  RAM 162
  RAMdisks 148
  requirements 81, 153, 172–73
  ROM 162
MEM program (DOS) 10, 15
menu bar 5, 7, *114,* 155
menus 6–7, 161. *See also names of specific menus*
messages, batch file 127–28, 129–30
messages, error 170–72
Microsoft Windows 148
minus sign (–) as Directory Tree operator 52, 166
Mirror program (DOS) 94, 109, 173
MODE command (DOS) 174
modes, display 5, 16–17, 133, 135–36. *See also* graphics mode; text mode
MORE (DOS filter) 92
mouse
  choosing list box items 12
  choosing menus and commands 7
  conventions 167
  copying files 30, 167
  editing text 8, 115
  moving files 31, 167
  pointer 5, *114,* 115
  selecting and choosing 6, 167
  selecting dialog box options 11
  selecting files 23, 167
  starting programs 65
moving files 31–32
MS-DOS Editor. *See* Editor program

MS-DOS QBasic (Main program group)
  on Active Task List 75–76
  described 13, 65, 156
  Editor and 172
  starting 67
MS-DOS version 5. *See also* command prompt (DOS); Shell program; *names of specific DOS commands*
  directory for 59, 60
  Editor (*see* Editor program)
  error messages 170–72
  features 1
  installation or upgrade 151–53
  QBasic 13, 65, 67, 75–76, 156, 172
  troubleshooting (*see* troubleshooting)
  version verification 4, 151

N

names
  directories 52, 54–55, 57–58, 61
  disks 43–44
  files 22–23, 32, 33, 52, 53, 89, 159 (*see also* extensions, filename)
networks 60
noise protectors 99

O

OLD directory 60
OLD_DOS.1 directory 153
OLD_DOS.2 directory 153
option buttons 10–12
options. *See* parameters
Options menu, Display command (Editor) 120

Options menu (Shell)
  Colors command 12–13, 135
  Confirmation command 15–16, *16*, 136–37
  Display command 16, 135
  Enable Task Swapper command 74–75
  File Display Options command 11–12, 25–26
  Select Across Directories command 24
  Show Information command 28, 38–39, 44
overwrite mode 117

P

parallel printers 93, 118, 161, 174
parameters 70, 84–85, 161
  used with Backup Fixed Disk 105, 106
  used with DIR command 84–85, 92, 93
  used with Restore Fixed Disk 107–8
  used with Undelete 109
parent directories 51, 52, 55, 90
partial backups 102
password protection 71, 110
PATH command (DOS) 53–54, 61, 144–45
pathnames 52–54, 61, 70, 88, 113, 144–45, 162
PAUSE command (batch files) 129–30
Pause key 84, 94
PC Tools 47
period (.)
  as current directory symbol 54, 55
  used with filename extension 22

PgUp (Page Up) and PgDn (Page Down) keys 6, 116, 166
pipe (|) 92, 162
plus sign (+) as Directory Tree operator 52, 166
pointer, mouse 5, *114*, 115
previewing
  colors 13, 135
  display mode 135
PRINT command (DOS) 92–93, 95
PRINT.COM utility 32
printer ports 93, 118, 174
printer problems 172, 174–75
printing files 22, 32–33, 92–93, 117–18, 172–73
print queue 95, 172–73. *See also* PRINT command (DOS)
Program/File Lists view 140
program files 22, 53
program groups 65, 68, 71–73, 77
program items 68, 69–71, 73
Program list
  adding program groups 71–73
  adding program items 68–71, 73
  deleting programs 73
  described 5, 13–14
  reordering 73
  running batch files 127
  running programs 13–14, 65–66, 72, 77
  views 140–41
Program List view 140, *141*
programs. *See also* files; Program list; Task Swapper; *names of specific programs*
  adding, to Program list 68–73
  backing up disks of 45
  directories for 59, 60

programs, *continued*
  running, from Command Prompt 68
  running, from File list 14–15, 66–67, 113
  running, from File menu 10, 45–46, 67
  running, from Program list 13–14, 65–66, 72, 77
  running, with batch files (*see* batch files)
  running multiple, simultaneously 74–76, 137
PROMPT command (DOS) 94, 141–43, 147

Q

QBasic interpreter. *See* MS-DOS QBasic (Main program group)
question mark (?) as wildcard character 24–25, 164
Quick Format (Disk Utilities program group) 42, 65

R

RAMdisks 148
RD (Remove Directory) command (DOS) 89, 91
README.TXT file 115, 169
read-only files 40, 85, 162
rebooting 43, 76, 101, 143, 145, 148, 169
recovering
  deleted files 108–9
  disks 42, 46, 107–8
REM (REMARK) command (batch files) 128–29
RENAME (REN) command (DOS) 89

renaming directories 57–58
renaming files 22, 32, 88, 89, 170
reordering Program list 73
replacing text (Editor) 118–19
Restore Fixed Disk (Disk Utilities program group) 65, 107–8
restoring from backups 107–8
root directory 40, 51, 52, 53, 56, 61, 90, 162
Run command and dialog box. *See* File menu (Shell), Run command

S

saving files 22, 117
screens
  clearing 130
  colors 12–13, 120, *121,* 133, 135–36
  display modes 5, 16–17, 133, 135–36
scroll bars 5, *114,* 120
scrolling, controlling 84–85, 92, 94
searching for and replacing text (Editor) 118–20
searching for files 29–30, 87–88
Search menu (Editor)
  Change command 119–20
  Find command 118–19
  Repeat Last Find command 119
sectors, disk 37–38, *37,* 88
Select Across Directories. *See* Options menu (Shell), Select Across Directories command
selecting
  dialog box options 11–12
  files 23–25
  techniques 6
  text 8–9

serial printers 163, 174
SET command (DOS) 145
Setup program (DOS) 151–53
Shell program. *See also* MS-DOS
    version 5; *names of specific*
    menus and commands
  batch file to start 125
  confirmation level 136–37
  dialog boxes (*see* dialog boxes)
  display modes and colors 12–13,
    16–17, 135–36
  DOS command prompt vs. 79, 81,
    133
  enabling Task Swapper 74–76, 137
  File list (*see* File list)
  help 15–16
  menus 6–7
  Program list (*see* Program list)
  quitting 17, 76
  returning to, from programs 13, 17,
    68, 71, 76, 81, 94, 173
  running programs from 63–68
  selecting and choosing 6
  starting 3–5
  troubleshooting 169–75
  views 137–41, 147
  window 4–5, *5, 17, 21*
Shift key 9, 23, 71, 115, 116
Shift+Alt+Esc key combination 167
Shift+arrow key combination 9, 24,
    167
Shift+F5 key combination 165
Shift+F8 key combination 24, 165
Shift+F9 key combination 17, 81, 165
Shift+Tab key combination 9, 167
Show Information. *See* Options menu
    (Shell), Show Information
    command

Single File List view 137, 147
software-related data losses
    100–101
sort order, File list 11–12, 26
Spacebar 10, 24, 136, 166
static electricity 99
status bar 5, *114*
subdirectories 49, 51, 52, 61, 84, 85.
    See also directories
surge suppressors 99
switches. *See* parameters
SYS command (DOS) 106
.SYS filename extension 32, 163
system files 40, 44, 108, 163, 170
  backing up 106
  displayed 84, 85
systems, customizing. *See*
    customizing

T

Tab key 5, 9, 166
tab stops 120
tape backup systems 103
Task Swapper 74–76, 133, 137, 145,
    147, 173
TEMP directory 60, 145, 148
temporary files 60, 101, 127, 145, 148
text boxes 8–9
text files (Editor). *See also* batch files
  creating, saving, and printing
    117–18, 172
  editing 115–17
  filename extensions 23, 32
  opening 114–15
text mode 5, 16, 115, 135
TIME command (DOS) 83, 94, 169
title bar 5
toggles 7, 30

tracks, disk 37–38, *37*
TREE command (DOS) 89
troubleshooting
  error messages 170–72
  general problems 169–70
  printer problems 174–75
  Shell problems 172–74
.TXT filename extension 23, 32, 113
TYPE command (DOS) 88

U

Undelete (Disk Utilities program group) 65, 101, 108–9
UNDELETE command (DOS) 94, 101, 108–9
UNFORMAT command (DOS) 42, 46, 94, 109
user-related data losses 101
UTIL directory 60
utilities. *See also* Disk Utilities program group
  archival and compression 103
  defragmentation 40, 47
  directory for 60
  DOS 81

V

VER command (DOS) 4, 151
video adapters and display modes 135
View File Contents. *See* File menu (Shell), View File Contents command
View menu (Shell)
  All Files command 28–29, 104–5, 139
  Dual File Lists command 138
  Program/File Lists command 29, 105, 140

View menu (Shell), *continued*
  Program List command 140–41, *141*
  Refresh command 140
  Single File List command 137
virus protection 100–101
volume labels 42, 43–44

W

wildcard characters 24–25, 33, 85, 89, 95, 164
window, Shell 4–5, *5, 17, 21*
Windows, Microsoft 148
word processors vs. Editor 111, 121
wordwrap feature 111
write-protecting disks 44, 45, 101, 164, 171

X

XCOPY command (DOS) 103
X-ray machines, and disks 48

CARL TOWNSEND

Carl Townsend is an international consultant, lecturer, and author. He has written more than two dozen microcomputer books. Recent titles include *PC Tools Deluxe: Microsoft Quick Reference*, published by Microsoft Press, as well as *Mastering dBASE IV Programming* and *Mastering Excel for Windows*, both published by Sybex. He currently resides in Portland, Oregon.

The manuscript for this book was prepared and submitted to Microsoft Press in electronic form. Text files were processed using Microsoft Word and formatted using the Magna composition system.

Principal word processor: Debbie Kem
Principal proofreader: Deborah Long
Principal typographer: Lisa Iversen
Interior text designer: Kim Eggleston
Principal illustrator: Lisa Sandburg
Cover designers: Becky Geisler and Leilani Fortune
Cover color separator: Color Control

Text composition by Microsoft Press in Times Roman with display type in Times Roman Bold, using the Magna composition system and the Linotronic 300 laser imagesetter.

Printed on recycled paper stock.